ENI

"How refreshing that each woman recounts her life-altering spiritual transformation and shares her inner life with God. And how delightful that their sharing extended to an intimacy with one another that surpasses what men can accomplish among themselves."

—*Richard R., PhD (Sebastian, FL)*

"I was enthralled to read these personal accounts. I could feel my own desire for a deeper relationship with Jesus, which has now strengthened my commitment to my own sacred healing work. Thank you, Donna, for bringing this gift to light for all humanity. And deep thanks and blessings to these twelve women who so boldly defied all social and religious conventions of their time to follow their hearts and embark on something much needed in this world."

—*Bonnie K. (Oak Grove, MN)*

"Here we find a remarkable examination of the twelve women apostles. These are personal stories that speak to the truth, beauty, and goodness that Jesus was and still is today."

—*James L. (Fort Myers, FL)*

"The reader cannot help but feel deeply moved. This work brings about a newfound understanding of the historical role and value of women in religion and the distinctive energetic signature they contribute to human evolution."

—*Tara M. (Nashville, TN)*

"A unique first-hand understanding of who Jesus was and how he positively influenced others. These twelve very personal short stories shed light on a special moment in early Christianity."

—*Randy S. (Andover, MN)*

"This book is a collection of touching first-person testimonials. Imagine talking to someone who had really experienced Jesus in person. That's what it feels like to read Donna's account of the twelve women. I know these stories will touch a very tender spot in your soul when you read them."

—*Anonymous*

"Women with Jesus. Enlightening insight in this book. Read it."
—*Steven M., PhD, LCSW, Spiritual Counselor*

"Enlivens and reveals anew the love of Jesus and our Divine Mother."
—*Dave T, PhD (Acworth, NH)*

THE
WOMEN
WHO LOVED
JESUS

THE
WOMEN
WHO LOVED
JESUS

The Untold Story of the
Women's Evangelistic Corps

Donna D'Ingillo

Origin Press

Origin Press
www.OriginPress.org

ISBN 978-1-57983-062-5 (paperback)
ISBN 978-1-57983-063-2 (eBook)

Front cover design by www.thebookdesigners.com
Interior design by Carla Green, claritydesignworks.com

Printed in the United States of America
First printing: July 2023

CONTENTS

AUTHOR'S PREFACE

The four gospels in the New Testament narrate the basic story of Jesus' life, but they tell us little about his relationships with the women who followed him. These accounts briefly mention that Jesus had devoted female followers who stood by him to the end, including Mary Magdalene, Joanna, and Susanna. But we know even less about the role of his female followers after his departure. Paul's letter to the Romans (see Rom 16:1) briefly states that certain women had become ministers known as "deaconesses," and historians tell us this practice continued for centuries.

But very much remains a mystery. Exactly how did Jesus regard the role of women in his ministry and in the church? Did he assign specific tasks to them? Which women, other than those fleetingly noted in the Bible, were closest to Jesus? Which ones became leaders in the gospel movement after his ascension?

The Urantia Book, a profound modern revelation first published in 1955, has revealed for the first time the startling fact that Jesus commissioned a set of twelve female apostles. It also tells us extraordinary things about how Jesus regarded women's roles in society and in his ministry.

And now, seemingly in response to questions in the hearts of students of *The Urantia Book*, a much more detailed account can be provided about the twelve women Jesus appointed to his Women's Evangelistic Corps. According to the stories these women share in this book, their ministry especially focused on creating the social network of love and compassion that later evolved into the Christian church. In fact, when you read each woman's chapter, you will discover how their efforts became a crucial part of the new movement of believers in Jesus.

Theirs is a unique story, almost completely lost from history. In their eyewitness accounts of the dramatic events of those times, these unique women share how meeting Jesus changed their lives forever. And we discover how, as a result of this inner transformation, their devotion to loving and healing humanity became the driving motivation for their ministries during and after his departure.

Introducing the Twelve Female Apostles of Jesus

It is my hope you find that these women's messages speak to your heart and soul. You will learn that Jesus not only fostered profound spiritual healing and growth in each of them, but also that he liberated *all* women, for all time, to their rightful place as equals with men.

Jesus taught that women are equal in spiritual receptivity and in their ability to grow in God-consciousness. In this book, you will discover how—from the very beginning—women were regarded as on par with men both as ministers of Jesus' love and in the sacred work of spreading his gospel to the world.

As we all know, there is no hint in the New Testament of the central message of this book—the story of how Jesus ordained an evangelistic corps of women apostles to minister to women, children, the sick, and the aged. No mention is made of the twelve courageous women he trained and empowered to help create communities of worship, healing, and fellowship. Very little is even recorded in the Urantia Revelation itself of how central these women were in helping people receive Jesus' love for humanity, and how their ministrations led to the development of the early church.

But now this omission is coming to an end.

Until recently, women in general have been consigned to obscurity within the annals of history. Fortunately, today's worldwide movement to empower women has resurrected facts about the roles women have played throughout the general course of human evolution and in the religions of the world. This account of the Women's Evangelistic Corps is another example of such a story that has been recovered from obscurity. We can now trace how a group of women commissioned by Jesus to be his female apostles played a fundamental part in the establishment of his teaching and healing ministry. Their efforts were complemental to the work of the twelve male apostles, and together these courageous missionaries created a movement that became the world's largest religion.

The Urantia Book and the Women's Evangelistic Corps

I was first exposed to this exceptional group of twelve women through my study of the very lengthy Part IV of *The Urantia Book*, "The Life and Teachings of Jesus." The women's story can especially be found in Paper 150, "The Third Preaching Tour." This inspiring material provides a brief account of how Jesus first commissioned ten women as apostles, later adding two more. It describes who they were, why he ordained them, and some of the work they did based on Jesus' teachings. Here's a key part of that story as narrated in the Urantia text:

> Of all the daring things which Jesus did in connection with his earth career, the most amazing was his sudden announcement on the evening of January 16: "On the morrow we will set apart ten women for the ministering work of the kingdom."... It was most astounding in that day, when women were not even allowed on the main floor of the synagogue (being confined to the women's gallery), to behold them being recognized as authorized teachers of the new gospel of the kingdom. The charge which Jesus gave these ten women as he set them apart for gospel teaching and ministry was the emancipation proclamation which set free all women and for all time; no more was man to look upon woman as his spiritual inferior. This was a decided shock to even the twelve apostles. . . . The whole country was stirred up by this proceeding, the enemies of Jesus making great capital out of this move, but everywhere the women believers in the good news stood staunchly behind their chosen sisters and voiced no uncertain approval of this tardy acknowledgment of woman's place in religious work. (150:1.1-3)

These are the women identified in the Urantia text: **Susanna,** the daughter of the former chazan of the Nazareth synagogue; **Joanna,** the wife of Chuza, the steward of Herod Antipas; **Elizabeth,** the daughter of a wealthy Jew of Tiberias and Sepphoris; **Martha,** the elder sister of Andrew and Peter; **Rachel,** the sister-in-law of Jude, the Master's brother in the flesh; **Nasanta**, the daughter of Elman, a Syrian physician; **Milcha,** a cousin of the Apostle Thomas; **Ruth**, the eldest daughter of Matthew Levi; **Celta**, the daughter of a Roman centurion; and **Agaman**, a widow of Damascus. Subsequently, Jesus added two other women to this group—**Mary Magdalene** and **Rebecca**, the daughter of Joseph of Arimathea.

I was very moved when I learned from *The Urantia Book* that Jesus always regarded women as equal with men, and that he was disturbed by the marginalization of women in Jewish culture. Jesus fully understood the role of women in building a healthy and spiritually enlightened society. In commissioning women to the elevated position of female apostles, he sent a very powerful message to humanity that women enjoy the same status before God as men. Unfortunately, the original male apostles—and especially St. Paul—failed to ensure that subsequent generations would maintain this practice. As the church grew in the early centuries, the facts about these women's early roles were obscured in the written accounts or else entirely lost. Here's how *The Urantia Book* puts it:

> This liberation of women, giving them due recognition, was practiced by the apostles immediately after the Master's departure, albeit they fell back to the olden customs in subsequent generations. Throughout the early days of the Christian church women teachers and ministers were called deaconesses and were accorded general recognition. But Paul, despite the fact that he conceded all this in theory, never really incorporated it into his own attitude and personally found it difficult to carry out in practice. (150:1.3)

Since the publication of *The Urantia Book*, this incredible information has fostered a keen interest in these special women. And today, women are finally taking their rightful place in religious work all over the planet. I believe we have earned these updated accounts, narrated in their own voices by the very first women apostles.

The Twelve Tell Their Story

This book is the result of my own contacts with each of the twelve women over many years. We are publishing it now because they want their stories to be known to the world. They have observed how modern changes within Christianity are finally bringing about more parity in gender roles. They are releasing their stories now because this long-awaited transformation has prepared the church to receive this lost knowledge. The "Twelve," as I often call them, are in a better position than ever to set the record straight about Jesus' historic relationship with his leading female followers, as well as their relationship with the male apostles and the early church.

It does happen that I am the conduit for this information. But this book is about something far bigger than my role. Please set that aside and instead focus on the content and plausibility of these stories. As you read each unique chapter, you will increasingly learn that this book is about the healing of our world. It also points to you, dear reader, and how you can play a role in this mission. In addition, it's about today's global movement for empowering women's roles as leaders in all sectors of society, especially in religion.

With regard to the future role of women in religion, this book offers a call to women everywhere to take on the helm of spiritual healing and all other forms of ministry for our world. Each of the Twelve were healers or teachers of some kind, and today you and I can follow in their footsteps, each in our own way—along with support from our male colleagues.

For those of you with leadership skills, one way to answer this call is to create your own Corps of like-hearted and like-minded sisters to uplift humanity, which is something the Twelve have inspired me to do. See the epilogue to learn more about that option for those who are ready to take up the religious challenges of our time.

In conclusion, Jesus' teaching and healing ministry was not just for his day—it is timeless and universal. The women's stories speak of human needs in their day that are similar to those faced today. But I believe these needs are now even more pressing than in the time of Jesus. For the sake of our survival, we must remember that we are sons and daughters of loving Creators and recognize the worthiness of our human nature. Just as in the ancient past, Jesus still heals our inner wounds and sets us on a course of spiritual living so that our God-given potentials can thrive.

May the words of these twelve women touch your heart, stimulate your mind, and awaken your soul. These twelve women shaped history behind the scenes. It is time for their stories, once lost to the world, to uplift all modern men and women. May these stories inspire us to expand our personal relationship with Jesus and lead us to be healed, just as it happened to "The Women Who Loved Jesus."

Donna D'Ingillo
Delray Beach, Florida
May 20, 2023

THE WOMEN'S INTRODUCTION

Jesus brought each of us into life, strange as this may sound. The Master was the living embodiment of abundant life. He radiated a magnetic drawing power that was always renewing and refreshing and full of joy and meaning. He generously shared these and many more lovely qualities with us, and we now reveal our experiences with him by sharing our stories as members of the Women's Evangelistic Corps.

Jesus liberated us from a tightly controlled religious environment. Before we met him, we did not even know we were so highly regimented in our daily activities. And it is unfortunate that this condition still exists for many women on your planet.

As you read our stories, you will learn what occurred in our initial encounters with Jesus, how he mightily drew us to him by the truths he spoke and because of his loving heart. He made us feel that we are worthy as individuals and as daughters of God. Jesus was able to look behind the influence of our culture and see into our souls, sparking in each of us an inner recognition of who we truly are. We now felt empowered to live up to the potential God had placed in us as his daughters. To imagine that we would not want to learn and be around this man was inconceivable to us. Over time it became clear that we would willingly devote our entire lives to him and his living gospel.

Our account focuses more on our spiritual experiences with Jesus and our collective ministrations to his followers rather than on the material aspects of our activities. This more religious focus is far more important, especially because our group dynamics formed the foundation of early communities focused on spiritual growth that later became the Christian church. Because your culture spends far too much time on material pursuits, we see a great need to help you recognize a higher path. We cannot emphasize enough how much joy we experienced through being dedicated to serving others, especially when we fed their souls as Jesus taught us to do. As you will soon see, the joy of serving is one of the main themes of our story.

Just as important, our growing understanding of who we were as women helped us open our hearts to a recognition of the Divine Mother, who represents the nurturing and life-giving qualities of all creation. For example, we had been trained to think of our bodies as ugly and impure, but Jesus taught us that our Holy Mother Spirit loves our physical feminine natures. This revelation liberated us in a way nothing before was able to do, and we began to honor our bodies and regard them as holy vessels. We also learned that we had unique value as women in the collective sense; this uniqueness, which set us apart from the male apostles, was revealed especially in how we socialized with one another in our Women's Evangelistic Corps and with those to whom we ministered. Jesus infused us with the power of the Divine Mother's Holy Spirit, setting us on a new foundation for ministries that were for the first time based on her love and how she upholds life. We felt empowered to create a fertile environment that enabled growing communities of believers to thrive from our ministrations and then go on to share the fruits of their spiritual growth with others.

We eventually developed a replicable model that greatly influenced the early socialization of Jesus' gospel. And the time is now ripe to return to this same approach today, so that humanity may be removed from its self-created ideologies and instead become inspired to create a highly developed spiritualized global culture. This was Jesus' intention for humankind, and conditions are building for this same recognition to burn in the hearts of all people, often with women in leadership roles.

Your modern cultures need to recognize the interconnectedness of all living things. We were drawn to Jesus because he enlivened in us this sensitivity to the sacredness of human life. One aspect of this was what you might call "Father-Mother synergy," which he fully embodied. Because Jesus was so balanced, this created a stabilizing environment in which we could welcome and minister to all persons equally, recognizing the divine dignity of each man and woman. As this same recognition of equality grows in your cultures and is more fully practiced, his gospel will become the living guide for humanity to develop a moral and noble culture.

We recommend reading our stories in a meditative state, which will increase your receptivity. The spiritual energy that lives within our words is more apparent when your inner environment is most receptive. We encourage you to not interpret our stories right away, but instead to first allow some time for our messages to soak into your souls. To our modern-day sisters: As you enter this meditative reading, you are welcome to invite us to minister to you so that you may open more to the mothering energy we experienced during our ministry on earth.

The Divine Mother offers what you might call a gathering and harmonizing essence. Allow her to lay the groundwork for collaboration and teamwork that is devoid of ego concerns and placed more squarely on the intention for the highest good of all to prevail. We suggest this because the women of this planet need to develop a greater appreciation for the personality of the Holy Mother Spirit. We encourage you to emphasize this message about our Divine Mother as you share her love with women all around the globe.

We also encourage you to be open to a heartfelt relationship with Jesus. As you do so, give yourselves permission to move beyond the wounding caused by eons of male domination. Allow the magnitude of his deep love and respect for women to enter into and inspire your hearts and souls. Today many of our sisters are still living under very diabolical and misaligned energies that come from centuries of patriarchal indoctrination. And who is able to show them the safe and divine pattern of masculine energy? It is Jesus, of course. He can and will support each woman devotedly. He will heal the wounds all women carry—those scars of abuse that have been perpetuated from generation to generation. He is here to assist them to heal *all* of these wounds. It is time for full healing and reconciliation.

To our brothers, we extend the same invitation. Give yourselves time in meditation to draw close to Jesus in your heart so that he may share his perspectives about women with you. This will soften much of the inner bias still unconsciously held that prevents a greater understanding of the role of women as powerful contributors to society. Jesus will also help you appreciate how women can assist men in the cultivation of their spiritual potential. We also encourage you as men to develop a more devoted relationship with the Holy Mother Spirit, a deep friendship that will foster more meaningful contact with her. This will help you, our beloved brothers, to release any remaining long-standing prejudices. It may also open a door to a more intimate relationship with Jesus, who was extremely balanced in both his masculine and feminine attributes. Men of today need to soften their ego puffery and stand more humbly in the embrace of the Divine Mother. There they can experience the rich and vast domain of her presence that harmonizes all human relationships.

Enjoy our stories! They are shared with you in love—love of God, love of Jesus, love of humanity, love of all life. May you be uplifted as we were in him, our Creator. We are with you on the journey of bringing humanity and the planet back to abundant life as so expertly demonstrated by our Master—the Living Jesus.

"His words had eyes and those eyes saw the soul."

1

AGAMAN

My name is Agaman, and my story begins long before I met Jesus. Like many of my time, I was enmeshed in a materialistic view of life. As a result, I felt an emptiness I could not quite satisfy through my relationships with my family and social acquaintances. I was married to a wealthy man who treated me well, but I was not especially interested in his pursuits of material gain. Those were his main interests in life, and I had to honor his choices because he was—in words you may abhor—my lord and master. But I was well treated, and I did experience a profound sense of loss when he passed.

It was shortly after my husband's death that I first met Jesus. The chords of my soul were immediately struck by an enormous emotional response, which I have now come to identify as the call of Spirit. At first, it was hard for me to believe that this man was genuine and sincere, but that was only my skeptical mind at work. At a deeper level, my soul was touched and something within me began to stir and quicken.

Jesus was an oddity for me in many ways. First and foremost, he struck me as unusual because of the way in which he spoke to women and to me in particular. He seemed to be moving into that place in my heart where my husband had once resided, yet in a more expansive way. His presence was so very different, unlike anything I had ever experienced before with any other man. At first, the emotions I experienced were confusing because his impact on me was so much more encompassing than anything I had experienced with my spouse.

The profound and energizing love of Jesus

Jesus' presence was such a stark contrast because of the love emanating from the very core of his being. This was a deep love, a profound love, an energizing love, and it changed me forever. It wasn't until I experienced this love from Jesus that I truly began to understand what love really is and how it can change a person. Before that, I think I was only half alive.

Prior to meeting Jesus, I don't think I understood what it meant to love freely and whole-heartedly. The reverberations he sent into my heart struck a chord so deep that I did not even know feelings like those existed until I felt them with him.

How can I explain this to you with mere words? The physicality of his loving presence was so dominating upon my heart that my whole worldview changed, and I knew I had to devote my life to him as best I could. Allow me to share this with you now, dear reader: Let your faith in Jesus open your heart so you too can receive what I felt. Let yourself be impacted in the way he changed me. I share this with you now!

What drew me further into his circle of influence was the way he spoke to women. When I heard him teach in a public forum, he would make eye contact with women who were standing off to the side or even sequestered behind a screen. It was as if his words had eyes and those eyes saw the soul. Those words went right into a person's soul. Can you imagine my disbelief when I really began to realize what he was doing and saying? I went through a time of great questioning at first, but I had to admit that he touched me in my soul and spoke the truth.

After I had time to adjust to this deep bond of love, I began to look at my life quite differently. You might say in your modern vernacular that I experienced a 180-degree change. After my husband died, I realized I had invested a lot of my own self-concept into how he treated me. In fact, I had what you call an identity crisis because I really didn't know myself at the time he passed. For, as you well understand, in our day women's roles were so narrowly confined that we had to base our identity upon this sort of social contract with our spouses as opposed to the direct inner relationship that one can have with the Creator.

At first, my disbelief in what Jesus had done in me so suddenly required time to adjust my identity and self-awareness. But as I continued to allow his presence to stir in me, more and more, little by little, I felt something new and irreversible coming to life. I knew I had been changed and that I would spend the rest of my life helping people achieve the same inner awareness Jesus had evoked in me.

Ministering to others at a soul level

The added effect of Jesus entering my life changed my perceptions of others. I began living my life in a larger context. I was lifted out of my husband's realm of materialism and began to glimpse the inner spiritual dynamics of working with individuals at a soul level. Over time, just being around Jesus fostered those intuitions that helped me see my brothers and sisters as children of God.

As these feelings deepened within me, I became a better practitioner at ministering to others. I am faltering with my choice of words because it is very difficult to convey these emotional experiences through the mere medium of language. The language of love is very different from a verbal exchange of concepts and experiences. In any case, what is most needed in your time is to convey this "language" as best you can, moment by moment. I was very fortunate that I could come into the presence of Jesus when he was near us and simply absorb that love. No words were exchanged. It was simply the experience of the joy of being close to him that expanded my capacity.

And so, as I grew in this expansive quality of love, I become more effective in helping my brothers and sisters find that same inner place within them. And this is the role of true healers today. So many people are searching for this feeling and are hungry for it but are not finding it. But you who are reading this story are fortunate in that you have access to the living Spirit of Truth that Jesus bestowed at Pentecost. This endowment conveys something of tremendous value to human spiritual growth. I encourage you to find the presence of Jesus within that leads to understanding his true gospel: the Parenthood of God and loving service to the family of humanity as an experience of living faith.

Over time I made contact with the other women—my true sisters, sisters in Spirit, sisters of heart and soul. We were all so different, yet we enjoyed a bond of sisterly kinship. Each of us had unique, edifying, and uplifting experiences. When we came together to share these experiences in group meetings, our kinship drew us closer and then even closer as the days proceeded toward his crucifixion and resurrection.

When I began to collaborate with my sisters of the Women's Evangelistic Corps, you might say that the combined synergy of our emotional awareness of the divine dignity of the other people around us was heightened. And from this place it was very natural to desire to minister to others, to ease their sufferings of mind and body, and to help them touch that spot within their beings where they could feel the presence of the Spirit.

My improved personal relationships with others, in turn, helped me perceive even more of the quality of love that emanated from his being—and as a result, I was growing even more in my ability to relate to others. It was so touching and so beautiful to see how people responded to the mere act of being loved in this way. My earlier experiences with my children also helped me minister with that same parental loving approach that Jesus taught us.

All this helps explain why the Women's Evangelistic Corps was so successful. Of course, our brothers, the male apostles, were equally changed by Jesus. But they did not have the same heart relationship to one another that we had among ourselves. That's why our collective work was considered to be very productive at introducing souls to the inner reality of God as their Spirit Parent, the idea at the heart of Jesus' gospel message.

So, you see, this was a wonderful time, a time when my life truly began. Because I had raised children and my grandchildren were of an age to be more independent of my influence, I was able to give my life fully over to the ministry of the Women's Evangelistic Corps. And it thrilled me to no end!

This is not to say that our work was easy because there were many individuals who were still very skeptical. Especially after Jesus left us permanently, we did feel a great void. However, after the Spirit of Truth was poured out at Pentecost, we were invigorated once again to share the message and to help people recognize who they are as sons and daughters. While we did have success in this work, it was hard-won on the battlefield of coming against the social and religious doctrines of our day and time.

My story is simple but I believe it is profoundly far-reaching. The circuits of the heart are infinite. In your world today, these pathways are being stretched and strengthened through the agency of the Holy Mother Spirit. She is helping her children become aware of what is available through these circuits, which are able to convey the exquisite energies of love.

Jesus is "the bread of life"

To close this sharing of my experience with Jesus, allow me to expand on his exhortation that "I am the Bread of Life." When he spoke these words, I experienced a very profound sense of personal empowerment that I had never, ever felt before.

Jesus conveyed a kind of spiritual substance through the transmittal of word-energy. This substance was very real but was not physically tangible. The traditions of the Eucharist in your Christian religious traditions are an interpretation of this experience of the "Bread of Life." Many people do indeed feel the spiritual value of this ritual; they actually perceive that Jesus is there inside of them, holding them up in a profound way. It is my hope that more people on earth meditate on this special quality, for this is food for the soul— that budding inner presence of your true nature that requires spiritual sustenance to grow.

Jesus as the "Bread of Life" can provide this sustenance through direct experience. Irrespective of whether you participate in the ritual of Holy Communion, or the Eucharist, as it is known in Christianity—this experience is real. I encourage all who read my account to simply focus on these words of Jesus as the "Bread of Life" and let him minister this truth within you.

What I have shared will suffice for now. It is not so important that you hear my whole life story; you only need to know of my spiritual experiences with Jesus. He changed me! He awoke the Spirit within me and I was forevermore changed. And the way to him is open to everyone. In him you will find your own inner truth of the spirit-presence within. And how touching, how endearing will that experience be when more and more of you deepen your soul recognition of who he was as a human, and who he is now in his divine persona. May he bless you on your journey, dear reader, and be a balm unto your soul.

"It was like an arrow shot from his mouth
and pierced my heart."

2

CELTA

Greetings, dear reader! This is Celta. I am pleased to approach you with my experiences as a member of this august group that Jesus commissioned. I begin my story with a brief background of my early years.

Because my father was a Roman centurion stationed in Palestine during the time of Jesus' life, I grew up in an environment of what could be called "social hostility." There was great resentment of the Roman presence in Palestine, especially among the Jewish people, and as a result I experienced a type of social ostracism that was deeply troubling to me. I did not grow up with feelings of self-worth or a clear sense of who I was. Nevertheless, I had within me a spiritual hunger that ultimately led me to find and follow the Master.

Palestine in those days was a very raucous place. I was raised with other children of Roman parents and was involved in carrying out domestic duties as part of my training to be a good Roman wife and mother. My childhood was limited to encounters with female friends and sister siblings that enabled me to learn about the chores and responsibilities that would become part of my future life.

While I knew this would be my role, I was rebellious at heart. I did not relish the prospect of my future as a Roman woman. I did not dream of being married one day as so many of my friends and sisters did. However, I had to succumb to the social pressure that made this sort of future inevitable.

As I was approaching my early womanhood, I listened as my father began to relate stories to his friends and my mother about "Jesus the rabble-rouser"—this strange individual who was going through cities and rural regions preaching and teaching a message of God. He said Jesus had stirred up quite a bit of interest, which naturally spread out into all areas of Palestine. It even extended to the Roman rulers, who looked into what he was doing to ensure that the peace was kept.

At that time the Jewish liberation movement was highly active, and the Roman legions were on guard to squelch any rebellion. When we began to hear accounts of Jesus, the natural tendency was one of suspicion that here again was another agitator who was fomenting the political aspirations of many individuals.

As my father recounted the stories he was hearing about Jesus, my natural curiosity was piqued. When I discovered that he was going to be speaking near my home, I convinced one of my sisters to join me on an excursion to hear him. When we arrived at the place where he was speaking, we found a rather large gathering. It was difficult to hear him at times, but the wind carried some of his words and we were able to pick up messages of spiritual import. And when I did hear certain of his words, it was like an arrow shot from his mouth and pierced my heart.

Something opened. Something in me recognized what he was saying. He struck a part of me that I recognized as real and truthful. I did not share any of this with my sister because it became clear to me that she only had a very fleeting interest. I was intrigued, so I sat with what he said for some weeks before he returned to preach in an area near my home.

As his words deepened within my heart, I began to notice flutterings of feelings that awakened in me. I believe what I was experiencing was the opening of my soul to the deeper yearnings of my heart, feelings that I had long repressed due to the conditions of my culture and the expectations of my family.

I pondered this for many, many days and weeks, and even months after I initially heard Jesus because I was so torn between my inner yearnings and the social pressures coming from my parents. They wanted me to marry as I was then of the age when it was my social responsibility to act as an obedient and productive Roman wife. I struggled with this expectation, and it took an act of great courage on my part to seek out the Master, to learn from him, and eventually give my life over and follow him.

I choose to follow Jesus rather than Roman tradition

You see, what I experienced was the love he awoke in me, and I wanted this at all costs. I was willing to give up everything to follow him because this love was so strong. Now, I knew my parents had affection for me, but the love from Jesus was so different; it was so profound that it allowed me to set aside all the conditioning of my culture, including the social responsibilities that had been foisted upon me. He was able to cut through all that. It did not happen all at once, but when it became fully alive in me, I was able to change my life forever and follow him.

During my initial phase of adjusting to my first encounter with Jesus, I had plenty of time to ponder what he said. I was able to contrast his teachings with the religious traditions of the Roman panoply of gods and goddesses that my family worshipped. One of the things that resonated so deeply was his approach to Deity: his message that each person already has the Kingdom of God within and can have their own personal relationship with our Heavenly Creator. You can imagine my dismay when I compared this with what I had been raised to believe. The vast assortment of deities presented in the Roman tradition was so complex and convoluted. Something in me resonated with the very different approach offered by Jesus.

As I continued to ponder the difference, I began to turn away from the worship services conducted by my parents. At first, they were not very happy that I was moving in a different direction. But as long as I was obedient to their other rules and regulations, they relaxed in their approach to my religious beliefs and started to give me more space to explore. You might consider this to be quite unusual in a Roman household because girls were trained to be obedient to their parents, particularly the father. My father was physically and emotionally distant for a variety of reasons, so it fell upon my mother to keep me in line, so to speak. But fortunately, the changes taking place in me began to also resonate in her, and whenever the Master was in our locale, my mother ventured out with me to listen to him as well.

My mother and I had many discussions about what Jesus taught. Some of these things were easy to comprehend, but others needed very deep consideration. Over time I became more comfortable with how he spoke to my heart. And it was at this time that I approached the women who were very close to him and started to ask questions. I would often sit with them for quite a long time, and just the act of listening to them had a profound effect on my thinking. He had liberated them from so much of their cultural conditioning and it started to rub off on me.

I witnessed their devotion to him. The love that existed between him and them was something that you could actually feel—almost like electric sparks moving between them. As I became more comfortable in sharing my inner life with these women, they began to help me feel the love that Jesus had for them.

Then one day, one magnificent day, I stood right before him. He called me by my name, and his heart drew me in. Now, this was not a physical embrace, but it could have been because the energy was so strong. I was still unable to understand his appeal because of my social conditioning, but it struck the same chord as before, and something in me truly awakened. I have since come to identify that place as my inner sense of what is just, right, and good.

I continued to discourse with the women about the teachings. They helped me understand the difference between my duty to God and my obligations to my family and culture. They showed me how to bridge the gap between living in these two worlds. And as this understanding deepened, I found my true path and made the life-changing decision to follow Jesus.

It was not something that came all at once, but when it truly solidified into my thoughts and feelings, I was able to stand firm and fast in my decision because I knew it was right. I knew this new life was true and real. So I struck out on my own and I followed him.

You might imagine the dismay in my family when I shared my decision. My mother cried. My father showed scorn. But I still felt their love even though this parental disapproval was their initial reaction.

I remained firm in my resolve, and one day I sought out and asked the women if I could join their ranks. This was before Jesus commissioned them as the Women's Evangelistic Corps. It was the early stages of their work and they embraced me in love with no hesitation on their part. They opened their arms and hearts to me freely even though I was considered the enemy because of my Roman status. They invited me to enter a love relationship. And enter I did! I had no regrets whatsoever about my decision.

I had many more direct personal interactions with Jesus, and each time I grew tremendously in my Spirit. How can I describe his love to you? It is something each of you can experience if you wish. I was fortunate in that I could benefit from direct physical contact with him. But now that his Spirit of Truth has been gifted upon all humanity, everyone has this ability to feel him, to learn of him, to know him, and to experience an intimacy that is beyond mere human understanding.

I am so grateful to share my story about how my experiences with Jesus became such a part of my soul and filled me with great joy. He opened me to a brand-new world—a world full of love and peace and goodness. And even though I still had to face some inner demons and unwanted outer cultural influences, he held me strong and steadfast. And this experience with our Master is the same for everyone. He is the foundation. He provides that inner foundation upon which each human soul can grow.

In the course of my deliberations on his messages, I felt an internal turning to the truth that resonated in my body and sparked feelings of hope and joy. This was a new experience because joy was never a regular part of my emotional life. There had been many times early on when I succumbed to feelings of resignation about my future fate as a Roman wife. Yet when this new-found sense of hope and joy became internalized, I was able to follow him completely—devoting my life to his ministry in whatever way I could.

My parents were shocked. They actually forbade me to move forward with my commitment to Jesus, but I was adamant. Now you might consider this to be a very dangerous circumstance, but I felt such inner peace that I was able to forge ahead with my decision. In time my parents could see the positive change in me and they relented.

I obtained their permission to meet with the women close to Jesus. I invited a few of them to meet my parents to allay their fears and misgivings about my decision to follow him completely. Mary, Joanna, and Rebecca came to visit with my parents in our home and they were very instrumental in convincing them of the purity of Jesus' heart. They also explained that Jesus had sequestered the women's ministry and how most of our ministry was done with women, children, the elderly, and the infirm. This assured them that my virginity would not be compromised—a great fear on their part.

They also allayed my parents' concern that I would not have what they considered to be a normal Roman life. As I said, I was quite satisfied to not follow that path. Once the women had fully conveyed the safety and security of what Jesus had to offer, they were more comfortable in giving me permission to strike out on my own and become a part of the women's camp.

So, one day I did! I said goodbye to my family, but not with the intention that I would never see them again. It was merely to say that I was taking up a different lifestyle and would be back to visit them from time to time.

My heart was full of joy when I formally entered the female camp of Jesus' followers. The women were so eager to welcome me, and it was almost immediately that I felt an endearing feminine kinship that was a new experience for me, one that I relished with great joy. They spent a great deal of time with me to share what they had learned from the Master and explain how I might find my own gifts in communion with my Spirit so that I could begin to work with them as a group.

My training in ministry and healing

There were times when I had very profound encounters with Jesus. My heart was always full of joy when this happened. It wasn't as if I needed a lot of time in front of him because the love that emanated from his heart to mine was strong enough to sustain me during those periods when he was not in direct proximity. When he was present with us it enlivened me in ways that no other person could ever do. And it is the same for you! Just invite him to take residence within your own heart.

Once I joined the women's camp, I quickly became acclimated to their spirit of service and ministry. And at first, I was quite surprised at the amount of work that was to be done in serving those who were following Jesus.

It was shocking to be in the midst of so much human need. Physical suffering and emotional imbalances were very much the order of the day for those who came to see the Master for the healing of their ailments. Jesus carefully taught us that much of the healing he performed is done within what you now call "consciousness"—adjusting one's attitude toward life experiences having to do with their habitual perceptions and cultural conditioning.

In our time there were very many superstitions along with the many rigid traditions that I soon began to learn about within the Jewish culture. People had been greatly impacted by these traditional ways. It was quite liberating to see Jesus minister to such people by penetrating to the core of their identity and self-worth, helping them to realize that their worthiness was based solely on their relationship to God. He showed them that they did not have to be so beholden to all the rules and regulations of their traditions.

Another surprise was the cheerfulness of the women ministers when they helped individuals drop their disbelief in their own value. It was as if they were able to turn on some inner light in these people. I attributed this ability to their very strong connection to Jesus, who had turned on *my* own inner light. My heart opened to these souls, for I too knew what it was like to suffer in my own sense of self.

In my day, tradition-bound people suffered from very ingrained habits and ways of relating, but I see the same problem in your culture as well. For, you see, the need of the human soul is the same now as it was 2,000 years ago or even 20,000 years ago. Each individual needs to be loved and "seen" for who they are. What was so impressive about Jesus was that this was exactly what he gave to people. His love touched people in such a deep way that when I saw it in action, I was transfixed. Even so, many simply turned away in disbelief. But for those who stayed with us and became the core of his ministry—we were all mightily uplifted in our approach to life.

As I began to learn the ways of ministry, my heart was very touched by the level of deep and profound suffering before me. I truly had no idea how deep this need for love was. I saw it everywhere I looked. I was very struck by how patiently Jesus dealt with so many individuals coming to him for healing. They wanted an immediate effect, and while some were instantaneously impacted, others could not understand what he was doing for them. For our part, we did our best to minister to each and all. We gave them succor for their physical ailments and offered them companionship in their time of need.

Our experiences after the departure of Jesus

We remained tightly knit as a group of women after Jesus left us—but we certainly felt grief. We continued our ministrations, helping people find that deep place within where they could feel the Father's love. Many began to apprehend the deeper meanings of his teachings, which soon began to spread and form the foundations of the Christian religion. But I digress a bit here.

In summary, my initial experience within the encampment was a time of great joy, which contrasted with the pain and suffering felt by so many who came to see Jesus. It was truly a remarkable event to be in close proximity to him, to hear how he preached and how those words were conveyed to each soul. When he traveled to another location, we were left with the aftermath—those who had come to receive love as well as our ministrations of the body through the herbs and oils I had by then learned and often used to help with physical ailments.

At that time, of course, we did not understand the genesis or origin of disease. Also, as you might imagine, the sanitation was quite poor. It was a struggle because there were so many in need. We gave them hope, perhaps not for this world, but for the future wherein all things would be made clear and people would come into their wholeness.

In closing my account, I wish to impress upon you how the messages and physical presence of Jesus truly changed my life and made me a better person. It is difficult to explain the love that emanated from every fiber of his being. But it was real and I was one of the fortunate people to be a direct recipient of this gift of love. I can only encourage you who read my account to open your hearts to his presence and experience this most intimate of relationships. He will guide you through the maze of your emotional life and assist you in your mental adjustments to your planetary cultural climate, so that you may indeed come into the fullness of your true self and thrive as a human—just as I was able to do during my brief human life so long ago. Now in my more glorified form, I am so happy to share my experiences with you all. Thank you for allowing me to speak to you. I withdraw now. Be in his peace.

"In your day as in mine, material excess leads to a type of spiritual affliction. I suffered in this way until I encountered Jesus."

3

ELIZABETH

My name is Elizabeth, and I am pleased to introduce myself and share my experiences with Jesus and the Women's Corps. My special prayer is that you and I enter into a bond of grace because my story is deeply relevant to what your culture is now undergoing.

I was the daughter of a wealthy father who surrounded me in luxury. In those days, luxury meant lots of servants, plenty to eat, and fine clothing and personal adornment. My father lavishly bestowed these material gifts upon me as an expression of his love. He was deeply rooted in the old Hebrew belief that the possession of material wealth signified the grace of God's favor.

My father's generosity served and supported me well in my youth. But as I grew up, I began to sense that I was not only a daughter of my father. I discovered that I was my own person who had unique desires and dreams.

At first, I did not notice it, but as I matured as a young woman, I began to experience a gnawing feeling—a certain hollowness that could no longer be gratified by material things. All I knew was that I felt empty inside. At some point, I realized that all the finery that comes with a luxurious lifestyle was not enough to fill this inner vacuum.

Eventually I drifted into an identity crisis. It felt very uncomfortable and I had no idea where to turn. I did not know who would listen if I were to share my true feelings. Really, there was no one! My father had deaf ears to my concerns because of his stalwart adherence to the idea that his wealth was a mark of divine favor. My mother and my siblings could not help me either, so I remained lost and bereft for quite a long time.

I'm very aware that many of you today are experiencing similar feelings that something essential is missing. Filling this empty place within is truly a need of the soul that cannot be gratified by material expressions that adorn and glorify a person's exterior. In your day as in mine, material excess leads to a type of spiritual affliction. I suffered in this way until I met Jesus, who radically changed my disposition and outlook on life.

My first encounters with the Master

I first heard about Jesus through the rumblings within the Jewish community as he went about his public ministry. You cannot imagine what a stir he created within the various synagogues he visited to share his teachings. Before long, several women who had heard him speak visited our family and shared what they gleaned from his preaching. Hearing their stories quickly sparked a flame of hunger within me, setting me on a path of discovery.

When Jesus next visited my area, I ventured out with my family to hear him. Seeing him was one of the most electrifying moments of my life! It was literally as if sparks flew from his heart into mine. Initially, I was quite mystified by the intensity of my response, so for many days I pondered what it could mean. I had conflicting feelings because I was still under the influence of my material attachments and my father's traditional religious beliefs. Juxtaposed against these familiar feelings was this new experience of something highly enlivening and enriching.

I sought out other women who knew more than I and asked them: The Kingdom of Heaven within—what does that mean? His parables, his stories, what did *they* mean? A deep curiosity soon began to resonate within me, speaking to my heart and mind. From this point on, I began to seek Jesus out in earnest so I could listen and learn more.

What transpired for me next was a period of great inner change. The conflicts I had experienced at first yielded to an unknown dynamic within. Looking back, I now recognize that an inner voice was beckoning me to something quite majestic and wonderful. At first, I was cautious and did not fully trust this new feeling, but as I pondered it in my heart, it began to feel as if Jesus was speaking to me from a distance. He was forging a bond within me even though I had no idea where he was physically.

To say that my experiences with Jesus were life-changing is an understatement. Feelings of joy were springing up that I had never before experienced. I witnessed the same type of joyfulness in the women who had gathered around him and noticed that it carried a very palpable energy.

I don't mean to say that this joy and gladness was experienced at all times consistently throughout the day. It was rather like an all-pervading essence, something similar to a fragrant perfume that you could detect by a certain intuitive sense. This feeling was so magnetic that it brought us women together simply because it felt so good to be around Jesus. Our experience of his love also acted as a bond that shaped us into a cohesive group. I can't say I understood what was happening, only that I felt a drawing sensation pulling me in to join these devoted women. I longed to share what we were experiencing with others outside our group who themselves were drawn into the encampment for healing and spiritual ministry.

My life was very much altered from this point forward. I had not yet reached the time when I was to be married by my father's arrangement, so I had to seek his permission to engage with the women in the encampment. And I can tell you that it was not something easily won. I revealed to him that a change was occurring within me, growing feelings of love and joy that needed to be expressed. After a bit of time, my appeal seemed to touch my father's heart and he reluctantly, although willingly, gave me permission to join.

How joyful I was on that day when I entered the encampment wholeheartedly! I gave myself and my life over to Jesus as I joined this growing environment of love, joy, and service. At first it was a very emotional time for me, and I drew strength from the other women as I learned what was expected of me.

My journey from material wealth to spiritual discovery

Can you imagine my amazement at coming from a very wealthy household where I was always waited on and had every whim gratified, only to find myself serving others in a place of great suffering and neediness? It was quite shocking! Yet it was also very inspiring, which helped me stay the course even without the comforts of my former home.

Devotion to service became my creed, and being with my sisters supported me as I released the trappings of my former life. I soon became enmeshed in the energies of service as the motivating factor for my work in the encampment. All my efforts were then pointed toward the alleviation of human suffering which, as you know, occurs at many levels ranging from physical deprivation and illness to all types of mental and emotional aberrations as well as spiritual poverty.

It took time for me to adjust to this challenging work after growing up so sheltered. I now see that my perspective on life was highly skewed because of my privilege. I began to witness many things in the encampment I had never seen before. At first, I did not know how to be helpful, but my sisters who had more experience with certain types of ministrations taught me with great patience and care. I began to discover that I had a real talent for serving my brethren.

Thus began a period of tremendous growth—from learning how to deal with a variety of people in need, to understanding how Jesus approached people and drew them out, to being with my sisters and sharing our life stories and experiences. What a time and what an adventure I was having!

When I returned home to share my experiences, my parents were flabbergasted at how much I had changed. But since their own life experiences had also exposed them to the plight of the poor, they began to change their outlook. I helped them understand that poverty and illness are not signs of God's disfavor, but rather something caused by the disadvantages of an unfair society. Based on this realization, they gave me provisions to take to the encampment and money to procure supplies. Their generosity was a great gift on their part, and I was also deeply grateful for their support for me as a young Jewish female.

During my early association with the women, I underwent a period of training in how to minister in the Spirit as Jesus taught. This instruction was very important because the human problems and circumstances that were showing up in the encampment were sometimes quite challenging. Jesus taught us that each person needs to experience a deep validation of self, thereby activating within them the feeling that they are worthy to receive God's love and favor. He also explained that everyone relates to suffering in a unique way.

My training with Jesus and the women took time, and I did not master these ways of ministering until after Jesus had left and bestowed the Spirit of Truth. After Pentecost, I felt an inner swell of truth-light illuminate my mind—as if a new source of energy was turned on. This rich infusion transformed my work.

Initially, I worked with several women who were more adept at simply listening to individuals. And the more I learned to deeply listen to those who came to us, the more I felt compassion for their situations. My increased compassion for them catalyzed both my desire and my ability to help such unfortunate people.

I soon began to notice that I could perceive intuitively more of what a person needed to hear and receive. And this approach became the form of spiritual ministry that most appealed to my heart and soul. Physical ministrations for healing the body were of less significance to me than the work of alleviating the mental suffering of those who did not feel loved and appreciated.

Jesus strongly encouraged this type of ministration to the human heart and soul. As a result, I began to feel great delight in meeting individuals and learning their life stories. You can imagine what a departure this was after growing up in a very privileged environment where I was not exposed to such a wide range of human suffering and neediness.

Learning Jesus' masterful skills of personal ministry

When Jesus was in the encampment visiting, training, and ministering with us, I marveled at his skill in drawing out that which was most valuable within a person—the divine dignity in each individual that is there simply because they exist. Almost magically, the results Jesus achieved were immediate in terms of an individual awakening to something they had never before experienced.

I was not the only one to marvel at this form of ministry. We all wanted to achieve the high levels of spiritual communication Jesus demonstrated. So, I applied myself to this work, spending many hours simply sitting with people, holding their hands, and being a receptive container for them to share their life stories. I grew in my love for each individual as I learned more about them, but I also discovered more about myself because they were sharing feelings I also had, feelings I once thought unique to me. The more I ministered to people, the more I sensed the common thread of the need and desire we all have to be loved and appreciated. This remains true even though the circumstances of each person are unique.

Jesus understood the human condition very well. Even though he was a great man and many felt shy around him, he was still very approachable. No problem or condition was insurmountable for him. He always understood what a person needed, but he did not dispense his wisdom to those who were not ready. He knew some were there to deride him and that others were simply not willing or able to receive what he had to give. But most who came to the encampment were either highly curious or were experiencing a deep spiritual hunger and a great need for ministrations to ease their burdens.

The story I am sharing about achieving a compassionate outlook on the human condition is very relevant for you today. There is no difference in the need for compassion across time. Love is not something that is bound by evolution. Compassion is an innate state of being, and it was able to manifest in our ministries because of the loving environment Jesus hosted and catalyzed for us.

No matter where you are on your spiritual journey, if you are motivated by compassion, you can make an impression upon a person that helps them overcome their sense of unworthiness or fear of life. Jesus developed this ability in us through our relationships with him, thereby enabling us to share this compassion with others.

By telling you our collective story, we wish to encourage everyone who reads this to understand that compassion is the foundation from which all things proceed to align in the divine will. I was fortunate to learn this in my human life and to achieve levels of ministry that were far beyond my intellectual understanding. I encourage you to grow in this capacity by allowing yourself to be seeded within by our Creator for compassionate ministry.

When Jesus formally commissioned us, I was a new member of the group. He bestowed upon us a mantle of blessing and benediction to be ministers of his message of love—of his teaching that everyone has a right to a direct connection with our Creator. Irrespective of my newness, I believe he appointed me because of my enthusiasm. At this point, I was one hundred percent devoted to being of service to my brothers and sisters and to acting as a conduit of my own inner wellspring of love.

The resonance of Jesus' love was palpable and highly charged with compassion and affection. And yet, there was another element that influenced us that defies description because it was based on the sheer experience of being around a Godlike person. Once this divine influence was secured in me, I was able to bring forth an unstoppable flow of love that I was enthralled to share with others. It was both joyful and purposeful. Even though I was very young and new to the ministry, I was motivated to stay the course with the Women's Evangelistic Corps and determined to move forward no matter how it played out in our culture.

My skills in listening and perceiving the cause of human suffering and unworthiness became more advanced. At times it was very apparent to me what difficulty or pain was at the heart of an individual's situation. I would simply sit with that person and allow my love to flow to them. However, it was not exclusively my love. There was a distinct resonance of Jesus' transcendent love that I was able to transfer into the heart of another person in order to help them perceive an even larger inner truth. You cannot imagine how joyful I was when I saw a spark of recognition light up within a person's eyes as they suddenly understood some very fundamental truth.

Our experiences and challenges after the resurrection

The time approached when the plot to destroy the Master came to its final fruition. We drew strength from one another during that trying time of intense sorrow during his arrest and crucifixion but before the resurrection. On that Easter Sunday morning, when our sister Mary and other sisters came to us with the news that he was alive, you cannot imagine our joy! Because he appeared to us in a different form, a great veil of mystery was suddenly lifted about what happens after death. This amazing experience filled us with great hope and joy for our future life, even though more mysteries remained.

During the period after the resurrection and before Jesus ascended and bestowed the Spirit of Truth, the Women's Evangelistic Corps met to plan what we would do next. Some women decided to become traveling missionaries and teachers. Others felt inspired to remain where we were to support the growing ranks of believers. Many new people were curious because an inspirational energy had been seeded into the entire region as a result of so many unprecedented events.

It was time for me to re-evaluate my earlier decisions about serving the gospel mission. I focused on my devotion to Jesus and sought guidance from my Indwelling Spirit as to the best course of action. I was led to return home to my father's house, but things would be different now. With his permission, we opened the doors to our home so that we could receive those individuals—mostly women and children—who came for spiritual ministration and healing. Some of my sisters joined me, and we remained there for a time until the political environment became too unruly.

It was a time of great political turmoil, especially because of the rising agitation in the Jewish community against Roman domination. I was able to face the political unrest with inner peace and balance, drawing strength from the Spirit of Truth as well as our memory imprint of the life Jesus had lived with us. When I did experience fear, I would simply call on Jesus and he would be there immediately to support me. I encourage you as my readers to also invoke him during challenging times so that he may infuse you too with his spiritual energy.

I continued to collaborate with the other women of the Corps in our area. We were able to provide sacred spaces of worship, places of communion with the Spirit and with one another. We focused on nurturing a community of believers in the divinity of Jesus and his earthly message. As our efforts expanded, the Jewish ecclesiastical authorities became increasingly aware that these new groups were beginning to turn their backs on Jewish religious doctrines. For example, instead of tithing to the Jewish authorities, believers redirected their financial resources to supporting one another— especially those who were impoverished or sick. This trend became more disturbing to the authorities as our movement gained momentum.

At some point, the Jewish leaders began to collude with the Roman government, convincing them that we were a growing threat. We had no choice but to move to a safer environment to continue our ministrations and community meetings and to avoid reprisals from the various authorities. After several years, the tension grew so strong that it even engendered the animosity of the larger Jewish community toward the growing movement of believers in Jesus.

At this juncture, the believer community had not yet developed into the formal Christian church; our scattered groups were only its earliest foundations. What we set forth in this phase of our work was a structure of love and compassion for one another as a mutual support system. In addition, the Jesus movement began to spread into other regions as the male Apostles continued their traveling ministries, also working with women missionaries from our Corps in a joint effort to secure pockets of Jesus believers in other areas.

My life was short-lived but was fulfilling and greatly enriched with love. I gained so much understanding of the human experience through my association with Jesus and how he taught us to listen and to minister in the Spirit. After his ascension and the bestowal of the Spirit of Truth, I felt an enhanced perception of him that encouraged me to embark upon the venture of helping people understand the same power of the Spirit. During this period, I continued to spend many hours sitting with people, listening to their stories, and sharing love by simply receiving what they wanted to say.

It is difficult for me to describe how my immediate group was raided by enemies and how so much blood was shed. My life ended in such a violent way that I do not wish to burden you with it emotionally. But I met my death with faith, and I felt Jesus pull me into his embrace no matter what befell my physical body. He helped me make that transition, and I was able to walk into his arms, separated from what was occurring to my body. My death was my life's greatest test of faith.

As I look back and recall this period, allow me to say to you: Do not fear the passing of one age to the next. For what we were able to achieve is continuing to bear the good fruit that Jesus always intended—the Kingdom of Heaven within, the Parenthood of God, and loving service to the family of humanity.

I end my story here. May you be fortified in the assurance that the presence of Jesus is with you and steering this world forward. There truly is nothing to fear. Even though I underwent pain and suffering at one level, my faith in him was unwavering and I made the transition to eternal life with his love and assurance.

I am delighted to share my story so that you may grow in your relationship with Jesus. May you grow in faith and trust—that living, dynamic assurance that all is well. May you be held steady and strong as the current age yields to a brighter future. I ask Jesus to fill you with divine grace and fill you with hope and peace. I thank you for allowing me to share my experiences, and I leave you in his love. Farewell.

"What is most needed now is resurrecting the purity
of his teachings and his ministrations."

4

JOANNA

This is Joanna and I am very pleased to address you in this manner. It is important that the message of the ministry of Jesus be portrayed from a different perspective other than the New Testament and its various interpretations.

I was married to Chuza, the steward of Herod. This was an important position for my husband, who became embroiled in many of the palace intrigues though not necessarily by his own volition. During the time of his stewardship, plotting and corruption were part of daily palace life. I did not like any of this, of course. But I found it difficult to separate myself from these stories since my husband confided in me the experiences he had while catering to the needs of the king.

My initial experience with Jesus was profound. I first encountered him at the Temple in Jerusalem at the Sabbath service during one of the feast periods, when he was invited to speak. I was very intrigued, not only by his mannerisms and the easy way he conversed with the congregants, but also by the simplicity of his message. I was sequestered with many other women behind the screen within the Temple, but I could make out his personal appearance and saw the way in which he delivered his discourse in such a heartfelt manner. Intuitively, I felt he was sincere. He spoke from his own personal experience, which had the ring of authenticity. And his message really resonated with me.

At this time, he was starting to gain popularity and cultivate a distinct following. The political climate was very tense, especially with the Zealots trying to thwart Roman rule over Palestine. Meanwhile, reports were coming to Herod about this man who was going about the countryside preaching, teaching, and healing.

Jesus first enters my life

In Jesus I found a gentle soul, a soul that seemed to understand my needs. For, you see, even though I was married to a man of importance within the household of Herod, I did not like the environment because it was "toxic," according to the term you use now.

So, when Jesus entered my life, I began to sense safety in his presence, an inner security that was strong enough to fortify me against the environment of the palace. Now, this was a large contrast. Positions in the palace were not secure. People's places of favor with King Herod were not assured. You never knew when you would be coming before the authorities because of some petty infraction that might get you dismissed from favor.

I was deeply impacted by the palace machinations; political intrigue of this sort is not a pretty thing. It is based upon greed, self-centeredness, favoritism, and a type of obsequiousness that is disturbing to the soul. But I had to adapt in order to help my husband maneuver through the political climate so he could support our family. Needless to say, we did not always enjoy this predicament but it did serve the purpose of providing for our material well-being.

Even though I was associated with a member of Herod's household, I had my own private thoughts and feelings about Jesus as he moved about the countryside. In truth, my spiritual curiosity had been primed for revelation from the first time I encountered him.

Please understand that there was something very peculiar about him, not only in the way he spoke but in how he comported himself. He carried himself with a regal self-assurance wholly unlike the supposed kingship qualities of Herod. Jesus' bearing was honest and sincere, and it came from a place of inner peace and fortitude no one could disturb. You could sense a majestic energy emanating from him, which was why we willingly called him "Master." Because he was so redolent of these qualities, we were humbled to be in his presence. Yet we were also very uplifted because he loved us so much and freely conveyed that love to our hearts. Because of his composed and confident way of being, Jesus created a place of safety in me.

I grew increasingly curious about him and what he was saying. His words and demeanor were beginning to help me lay aside the disturbing influences on me from the palace conflicts. It was as if he lifted me out of that morass into a place of idealized beauty that deeply resonated in my heart. At some point, I began to feel like I was living in two worlds. The elevation of Spirit idealism that Jesus represented carried me through the challenge of palace life where I had to guard my behavior at every moment.

Eventually, I sought out those sisters who were most devoted to him. With their help I began to sense that my life was indeed changing, that I had to make choices not only about following his teachings but also supporting his ministry. This led me to a time of great deliberation within my heart. I was torn between my loyalty to my husband and my loyalty to Jesus. Fortunately, I was able to reconcile these two aspects. Jesus helped me realize that, while I did have familial obligations to fulfill, I could still assist the Women's Corps during my periods of free time.

The sisters begin to organize themselves

As time progressed, I became closer to the women who followed him. We began to formulate ideas about how to work together as a group to promote his teachings and support his ministry to the masses who came to hear him and who would be in great need of physical, emotional, and mental relief. We sensed the higher principles behind our obligation to our fellow humans, which of course was a central theme of the gospel teaching of the fraternity of all humanity and the need for loving service.

We began to consider what each woman's gifts were and their degrees of interest in forming a more organized group. At a certain point, we presented a proposal to Jesus. He assented and formally commissioned us as his female apostles, along with the assurance that we were on an equal footing and would enjoy the same privileges as our male compatriots. At the same time, he directed that we minister in a different way than the men did.

After Jesus had commissioned his twelve male apostles, they began teaching and preaching throughout the region of Galilee and its environs. Over time, these messages drew many out to hear him. This was especially the case after the healings Jesus performed became acclaimed throughout the region. You can imagine how this news drew even more of the curious and those seeking relief from their ailments.

As the ministry of the male apostles progressed, many more women became interested in what was occurring, particularly to ease the suffering of many who were in very dire straits in their bodies or minds. We women are nurturers and healers for our own families, and the suffering of these people naturally stimulated our desire to minister to those who sought out Jesus. For the same reason, several of us began to follow and support the missions of the apostles as they went out into specific regions.

Our efforts grew to the point where we began to organize in teams. These teams would perform specific functions, such as gathering alms for the materials we needed, which included food, shelter, and medicines such as oils and herbs that we used for healing. Joining one of these teams gave me my first exposure to the merciful ministrations of the women who were devoted to following the Master.

The Women's Corps was particularly interested in me because of my relationship with the court of Herod, which would allow me to pick up information relevant to helping Jesus spread his teachings. I could also find out through various means the things being said about him in the court. And so, I shared these facts and (what you might call) gossip about Jesus with my sisters. Some of these pieces of information we brought directly to Jesus. He was very respectful of what we shared but did not give it much weight. We sensed he already knew these things.

The Corps learns how Jesus ministers to those in need

As interest grew, many more people came to the encampment, and we became much more involved in ministering to these hungry individuals. When he was in our encampment we brought certain ones to the Master for teaching and healing, and we learned how he ministered to those in great need: the needs of the soul, mind, heart, and body. He seemed to perceive all of what was transpiring in a person's inner life. Sometimes he spoke not a word, but the love he conveyed from his essence to another person radiated a powerful surge of light that was almost perceivable—it was detectable by intuitive means.

It was very uplifting and inspiring to see how he went about promoting good cheer, even in the midst of some very difficult situations. He took his time with people, never leaving their bedside or telling them he was finished with them until he felt that they had received what they needed. He was generous, kind, and understanding. By observing him closely, we learned some very important lessons in ministering to those who suffered greatly.

I was most impressed by his compassion and the way he could find that place within a person he could touch to evoke a healing response. Of course, not everyone was miraculously or instantaneously cured. But he always fortified people in a part of their being that had heretofore laid dormant. He spoke to their soul; he revealed to them a quality of truth and realism that resonated deeply upon their soul. And from that point, an indelible mark was forever etched upon that person. It altered them, some more so than others, as some could not understand the deeper implications of what he did. However, all who came in front of him, even those who were his detractors, felt something move inside. This experience was accepted by some and rejected by others.

What your culture is missing: listening to the soul

One part of our story is vitally important for your day and time because it speaks to a type of ministry that is still very much underdeveloped in your current planetary culture. You might call it the culture of listening to the soul. And even though you have many types of therapies available to you that we did not have, we have one taught directly by the Master—the art of soulful listening and ministering the balm of love and compassion to each person.

Once this approach is better known on your world, his teachings will truly be resurrected. In Christian thought we often find a strong emphasis on the resurrected Jesus, and it is true that some people do have powerful experiences with him as the resurrected Lord. But what is most needed now is resurrecting the purity of his teachings and his ministrations. We hope that by sharing our account, more people will learn of this way and will wish to emulate it.

Our encampment was a hotbed of activity. A great amount of ministering was needed for those who came for spiritual uplift and the healing of their maladies. Our experiences as a group became more powerful as we learned how to share our gifts with one another. At times we bickered, as some women sometimes felt slighted because they could not always get as close to Jesus as they would have liked. But over time, and the more we learned and gained from him, these petty differences began to subside. We grew to respect and love one another as sisters in this beautiful family that Jesus was developing.

What life was like in the encampment

My involvement in the encampment was limited because of my home life with my husband and children. Still, I devoted as much time as I could to fostering interest in the women's encampment. I sent people and supplies there as best as I could. It made my heart glad when I was successful in getting the discarded excesses of the palace donated to the encampment.

I found it quite daunting and even overwhelming to witness the neediness of the common people of Palestine. Each individual had specific needs and the number of people who began to flock around Jesus was very challenging to manage. Fortunately, the male apostles had organized into working groups to attend to the masses. As we formalized our work, we followed our brothers' examples and organized in our encampment to become more effective in helping those who came to us for healing and succor.

When Jesus was present we ministered alongside him, which allowed us to appreciate the depth of his ministry. He touched people's souls and often gave them hope for a better life in the worlds to come. Jesus taught that the life process is a continuum and that a great gift of eternal life awaits us if we choose a life of the Spirit. This was quite a revolutionary message. His words were so poetic, and yet they denoted his great trust in the Father's love. He was a living example of faith in the afterlife as he demonstrated during his final hours on earth.

Before he left this world, we had learned to minister in the way he taught us, and this included ministry to those who were dying. Many people passed onto the higher realms during their stay with us, and we helped them find a certain level of comfort and peace so they could leave their human bodies without fear and with great anticipation of a better life to come.

At the same time, the encampment was also a place of great joy, as many parents came with their children. We played with the little ones and enfolded them in our love to help them deal with the situations their family members were facing. Many mothers brought their children to us simply so that we would hold them and allow them to feel the spiritual presence that emanated from Jesus which we were fortunate to also impart. As a result of these things, there was much laughter and gaiety amidst much suffering and sorrow. The encampment was a very dramatic place because of the wide range of emotions expressed there.

I experienced great joy in contributing support from the palace and in the other ways I helped my sisters in their work as healers and ministers. We each gave what we could and we bonded together in a very close-knit way over time, which was very uplifting for me. Of course, when the Master left us, we were all exceedingly sorrowful, but the comfort we experienced with one another—through storytelling, singing, and mourning—bonded us together in an extraordinary way.

In fact, we became more dedicated than ever to the ministry he so fully established during his human lifetime. We continued to help people come into a relationship with him and with the Indwelling Spirit Jesus had so masterfully taught us about, and which was a cornerstone of his gospel.

Who wouldn't fall in love with him?

To be around Jesus was an experience unlike anything else I ever encountered in my human life. It is challenging to put into words the qualities of his personality and those delicious fragrances of Spirit that he naturally exuded. When you were in his presence, you knew you were in the midst of something great and glorious. I grew tremendously in my spirit just from being around him. The pure emanations of his love were his gift to all who were open to receive him. It truly was a joy to feel the presence of his being enveloping me and to also realize that I could embrace its essence and share it with others.

When Jesus came to visit with us while we were ministering, there was excitement because he always carried a heightened attitude of pure joy in being alive. This quality strongly and richly vibrated from the essence of his being. Who wouldn't fall in love with him? Yet for those who had closed hearts and minds, they could not understand his appeal or why he was so magnanimous in his approach to loving people and speaking to their souls.

It was not so much that Jesus healed the body; more important was how he healed the soul. Invoking his presence in your day and age could do much to change the isolation, the abandonment, and the unworthiness so many of your modern-day brethren experience because of the lack of spiritual vitality within their lives. He is just as alive today as he was then, albeit his manner of communication is of course different than when he was in close physical proximity. And yet, physical proximity pales in comparison with his spiritual presence within each human being through his Spirit of Truth. What is most important in your era is that you have universal access to him without his physical presence. You may access him at any moment, any time, in any experience you are having that may cause you consternation or confusion.

What I experienced with him was this simple quality of love, which was so fundamental to maintaining my interest in sharing his message with my fellow brothers and sisters. Because each woman had her own version of this experience, we grew a familial relationship with one another. Our spiritual kinship and our unified and combined energies became a powerful force.

The power of Pentecost and the Spirit of Truth

When he left us permanently, we were very mystified as to how we would proceed. But because of the grace of Pentecost, we received his Spirit of Truth through the action of our Holy Spirit Mother. This great gift allowed us to immediately proceed from a place of great enthusiasm. We went forth again to share his message of fellowship as brothers and sisters in the family of the divine presence of God within.

As we labored together under this new infusion of spiritual vitality, we became more spiritually magnetic. We were able to draw more people to us who were being called by the Spirit to learn of a greater truth. Aside from Pentecost, another aspect of our rapid growth was the fact of his resurrection and his many appearances to us in a quasi-material state. Great acclaim was broadcast by the disciples and apostles throughout Palestine about his presence being among us once again, gaining everyone's attention. For, how could a person who was crucified and buried in a tomb suddenly reappear within our midst, speak to us, love us, encourage us, and above all, inspire us to generate that enthusiasm to share his message of love with the world?

So, you see, even though there is skepticism about who Jesus is and was, including his mission and purpose, he is accessible even now, and that is because of the great events we witnessed. I can only encourage you to go within and ask, "Jesus, show me the way. Speak to my heart and teach me your ways."

It is normal for the human mind to question such claims about spiritual realities. I encourage everyone who is skeptical to let go of what your culture teaches about Jesus. Simply seek the inner experience of knowing him intimately. He will proclaim: "I stand at the door and knock." He is always there because of his omnipresent Spirit of Truth. He is knocking on the door of your heart and soul. Will you answer it? Will you invite him in? Will you let his love become so fully vibrant that it naturally spills out from the essence of your being to share with others?

This leads me to the challenges of the current Christian church with all of its denominations and varied belief systems. Again, listen to the call that we of the original Women's Corps are making: return to a more simplified version of the Master's teachings. This can be best achieved through an intimate personal relationship through the Spirit of Truth. Remember also that Jesus thoroughly developed his Godly nature as a human. He was and is our inspiration— our role model.

According to the account of his life in *The Urantia Book*, the evolving Christian religion incorporated existing religious concepts, beliefs, and rituals of our day that did not really belong. These inclusions adulterated the original gospel message Jesus taught us to share with our brothers and sisters. Now is the time to return to the purity and the simplicity of Jesus' true teaching based on the family of all humanity under the parenthood of our loving Creator.

You well know that theological and doctrinal debate has long been a central theme in the evolution of Christianity. But what is missing now is the encouragement of individuals to develop their own relationship with Jesus. It was easy for us to do this because we lived with him. He was among us. But for you, there is insufficient attention to the direct experience of opening the door of your heart where he always stands, waiting to enter. Get to know him not only in his divine persona as Jesus the risen Christ, but also as Jesus the human brother who loved humanity to the fullest degree of his human potential, and who wishes to awaken that same potential in you.

This is a simple approach, but very challenging. The church is now beginning to yield to this higher concept of direct personal intimacy with Jesus. What a great time it will be in your world's history when his true teachings are totally lived by each individual! The human potential he cultivated was so attractive! His spirituality emanated from every fiber of his being! We hope this message is seeding your desire to strike out on that same path—to craft your human personality along these exquisite lines of Jesus' masterful ability to reach these heightened states of God-consciousness and spiritual living.

I end my story here. May each person who reads this account take this moment and simply ask the question, "Jesus, who are you? I need to know, and I ask you to show me the way." The way is open, the path is clear. What will it take for you to walk in assurance that he is ever more present to hold your hand and to guide you on this faith journey to the cultivation of your own beautiful inner gifts?

"He recognized that we had valuable gifts that were not acknowledged by our male brethren."

5

MARTHA

I am Martha, sister to the apostles Andrew and Peter during my human life. As I share my experiences with you, I wish to underscore how Jesus elevated human thought. That is, his ministry transformed what you now know as "consciousness." And yet, this work of moving people to higher levels of perception was not as easy during his public ministry as it was after Pentecost. Because he had bestowed his Sprit upon the whole world, it actually became easier for us to convey his teachings. Thanks to Pentecost, the Spirit within was now able to achieve harmonic resonance with the Spirit of Truth to help each person open to this more advanced consciousness of universe reality.

Please consider this fact to be a foundational point as I share my deep love for the Master. And bear in mind that our goal throughout was always to lay a spiritual foundation for the people who came to us. We especially helped them access their Indwelling Spirit to better perceive the love of the Father within.

My brothers, Peter and Andrew, introduce me to Jesus

My human brothers were rugged men. They were very manly in their approach to life. Thankfully, our immediate family was full of love, camaraderie, and respect for one another. At the same time, their respect for me was conditioned by our Jewish religious traditions.

As mentioned in the Bible and as explained in detail in *The Urantia Book*, my brothers met Jesus due to his association with the Zebedee family.[1] In our town of Capernaum, we all knew about Jesus because of that connection. As those who have read *The Urantia Book* know, Jesus worked with the Zebedee family and with my brothers as fishermen for a period of time. As a result, there were occasions when Jesus would come to our home to socialize with us.

Because of those visits, I began to sense who this person was. I was very drawn to him in a way that was new to me. It was not a physical or sexual attraction. It was something vastly superior to that, and more profound. I now understand that he was able to radiate a spiritual resonance from the higher levels of his own being. At that time, however, all I knew was that I was interested in him. I felt prompted to listen and absorb what he had to say.

He was a very robust individual, also very manly in his approach. But there was also a lovely gentility about him. I could sense a tenderness in the way he spoke with great compassion and concern. He made people feel as if they were important to him and had something of value to say. This

---

1 See *The Urantia Book*, 129:1.2-12. The figure known as "Zebedee" was the father of James and John, who later become apostles along with Peter and Andrew. All of them were fishermen in the Zebedee business. (See also Matthew 4:21-22 and Mark 1:19–20.)

struck me as quite unusual in a man, because even though my brothers loved us and cherished us, they did not convey the same level of respect to us as Jesus did in listening to what was happening in our lives.

When my brothers became his first two apostles, mighty changes occurred in our household. At first there was confusion and concern, as it was highly unusual for men like them to become devoted to a particular teacher. But once we discovered that there was something highly attractive and sincere about Jesus, our concerns were allayed. Of course, this was before we learned who Jesus really was and found out about his special mission to the world. All we knew at first was this was a very attractive individual so full of love and tenderness that we were all drawn to him. In fact, it was hard not to fall in love with Jesus.

As my brothers embarked on their journeys as his apostles, we wondered what would come from this missionary work. But when they returned home and shared what had occurred, I became highly curious. Before long they brought me directly to him, where I could sit and ask questions. In my initial meetings with him, Jesus ministered to me in ways beyond my understanding. Nevertheless, I felt its impact and was very drawn to him.

While my brothers provided my introduction to Jesus, my relationship with the Master was vastly different from theirs. This is to be expected because we are all unique individuals. But also, being that I am a woman, the Master was sensitive to my spiritual nature and much more responsive to it than my brothers. Jesus activated a certain characteristic that created a longing for goodness. But again, I did not recognize at first what he was evoking in me through the power of his personality.

Jesus commissions the Women's Evangelistic Corps

I then began to share my feelings and thoughts with other women who had begun to encircle him. As I grew more confident in my inner gifts, I became even more involved with this growing coterie that were so attached to Jesus. Some of them I had already known peripherally, but when we were commissioned as a ministering evangelistic corps, our relationships with one another grew tremendously as you might imagine. At the time, none of us understood that Jesus was building a community of individuals who were spiritually awakened.

A certain sense of validation and empowerment came from association with my sisters in the Corps. Our group energy fostered the expression of all our combined gifts in a unified "family," and this in turn was predicated upon the love Jesus had for each one of us and we for him. In other words, our experience of respect, love, compassion, and tolerance led us to a beautiful synergy. I now understand that the Divine Mother Holy Spirit embraces and shapes her children into groups that feel like families, which is so fundamental for the development of a healthy social order.

It took time to recognize my gifts. It was not something I felt all at once nor could even experience all at once. At first, I felt constrained within the confines of my religious tradition, but those tethers began to loosen the more my association with Jesus grew.

I shared with Peter and Andrew what I was experiencing, and they took in what I had to say. However, it was more difficult for Peter to appreciate my transformation than it was for Andrew; I had more of an affinity with Andrew than with Peter.

As the women became more unified, more of my gifts could be expressed and freely given. I found to my delight that I was not rejected; I was not marginalized in the way my culture had previously done to women. As a result, this became a time of tremendous inner growth as we all shared in the exquisite essence of the love in which Jesus held us. As I look back, I cannot imagine using another word other than being "held" in his love. It was a container. It was an essence. It was a feeling and a knowingness.

This is all a matter of experience, and we really did experience this love to such depths that we could all come together as one. Our oneness grew over time as we learned how to work together as a team. We shared our different opinions respectfully, and then we prayed together for divine guidance regarding how best to pursue our ministering efforts. All these steps are key components of the family kinship and community-building Jesus taught us. These practices bore good fruit, as demonstrated by the fact that we were able to attract many people to our encampments to receive the benefits of our spiritual ministry.

My experience with Jesus was unlike any other I have ever had with another human. To those of you who are readers of the Bible or *The Urantia Book*, all I can say is that I recommend you spend more time in communion with him. Let his love resonate within; let him empower you as an individual and as a member of womanhood or manhood. You will sense more of your true power because Jesus validates who you are at the deepest level of your being. It is perceivable. It is palpable, and when you receive this love you are forevermore changed.

I become a leader of group worship and fellowship

My association with the Corps brought out my gifts. I discovered I had the ability to act as a leader of group worship and to also bring people into the fold. And I was delighted by both roles. I was also very happy to share the good news Jesus was preaching: the communion each person could have with their own Indwelling Spirit that led them to enter the Kingdom of Heaven within. Later on, when Jesus' Spirit of Truth was poured out along with the universal bestowal of Indwelling Spirits, these gifts improved our work.[2] They transformed our mission to build a family of spiritual recognition of the kinship of humanity under the Parenthood of our Creator Father and Mother.

As I grew in the understanding of my own gifts, I was able to help others find theirs as well. I now believe this identification of the gifts of the Spirit was fundamental to the growth of the early church, although at first we did not identify it as such. Of course, there was no such thing in those days as the Christian Church. It was more of a family of believers in communion with the Spirit of God. This group experience held us steadfast in the times of turmoil that soon followed.

---

2 Learn more about this epochal phenomenon as reported in *The Urantia Book* in the section entitled "What Happened at Pentecost" at 194:3. See also Acts 1:1-7 in the Bible.

My role as someone who would draw other women into the fold was in part due to my association with my brothers, because there was a mystique about them being chosen by the Master. As a result, it was fairly easy for me to step into the role of leadership in bringing women to the encampment. This is not to say that I sought this role for myself; it just seemed to naturally evolve because people knew me as the sister of two apostles.

We learn to create community with the help of Jesus and Divine Mother

The decision of Jesus to create the Women's Corps greatly delighted us. He recognized our valuable gifts that had not been acknowledged by our male brethren. Jesus seeded this recognition into us, but it had its origin in Divine Mother's desire to use us to build community. I suppose the best way to put it is that we were empowered to grow a homelike environment for people to feel loved and nurtured. It was my role, but not exclusively, to help the new followers of Jesus feel at home with us.

Various factors came into play in the progression of our roles. We began as simple women ministering to the infirm, the elderly, and the children. But in time, we became a formal group that had more influence and power—spiritual power—to bring all kinds of people into the emerging community that later evolved into the Christian church.

We were loosely associated before our formal commissioning. We did not jockey for position. We did not strive with one another, although there were times when we were not in full congruence or agreement. Jesus always helped us harmonize thanks to his majestic personality.

Perhaps another factor was the quality or essence that all women carry of the Divine Mother, which enables us to act as harmonizers within a group. Many of us had been mothers, and it was our responsibility to teach the children how to get along with one another. This was something we had more experience with than the male apostles.

Here's a note of encouragement I want to direct to modern-day women: Become leaders in harmonizing with one another. Develop your relationship with the Holy Spirit and ask it to fortify that divine mothering impulse, that gathering and harmonizing quality that emanates from her divine personhood. It is already there within you. Now it is time for this ability to become more enlivened. Jesus wants this for his daughters!

The overarching presence of Jesus in our community was redolent of his love. We experienced a certain type of absorption into his essence that left a strong and indelible mark upon us even after he departed. And that was strengthened by the Pentecostal bestowal of the Spirit of Truth. He was with us in this new way! Until the end of our human days, he remained with us—we grew strong and courageous in a bond that was unbreakable. This special bond greatly supported us in the days of challenge and strife after we were scattered.

The influence of Jesus on us could be called "soul resonance." His soul was so vastly all-encompassing that it evoked a sense of deep reverence. Some might liken this quality of reverence to the act of worship—the impulse to come into a shared space to commune together in Spirit. This feeling stimulated the urge within us to come to the Creator of all with humble appreciation for our power as daughters of God. This same dynamic is still applicable in your modern culture as a very appealing and attractive "energy field," if I may use today's vernacular. At that time, we did not understand its principle as much as we trusted in what we were experiencing because we could see the fruits of it. We were all connected in this field of love and reverence. There was almost something magical about it.

I often served as a facilitator and leader of this reverential communion that expanded into group worship. And there was power in these worship sessions. There was genuine peace. And again, this faith-certainty was even further expanded when Jesus endowed us with the Spirit of Truth at Pentecost.

Developments in the Jesus movement after Pentecost

Before he left us in his glorified form, Jesus had established our encampment as the foundation for what later developed. Pentecost provided a mighty infusion that created, in certain pockets, growing communities of believers. We had not been aware of his previous travels throughout the Roman Empire during which time Jesus seeded his teachings in numerous remote regions, including Athens and Rome.[3] As our worshipful and communal congregation grew in Jerusalem, it was as if what we were experiencing was transferred through the action of the Holy Spirit into these other receptive areas. When the male apostles went out on their adventures of

---

3 This story is revealed for the first time in *The Urantia Book* in Papers 130 and 132.

preaching the gospel, the field of receptivity had already been prepared in many places.

Here is my recollection of what happened after Jesus left us. During the period intervening between his resurrection and ascension, there were attempts at creating an organization to promote his teachings and the energies of this love. Please keep in mind that everyone did their best, but there were misunderstandings in certain quarters.

For me, it was a time of testing of my faith. Without the physical presence of Jesus among us, all of us experienced a vacuum. The rudder of spiritual direction he provided disappeared almost overnight, and of course we were also dealing with our grief over the way he was horribly treated and executed. And so, in this period between the resurrection and the ascension, we were still operating in a very unusual type of uncertainty. I had no choice but to explore my own desires, intentions, and motivations more deeply, and many of my sisters did this as well.

After this pause, we came together once again as a community of believers in Jesus and his special earth mission. During this period of discussion and group introspection, we again began to feel a common bond growing within us. At the time, the women were still formally organized as a ministering group. As we continued to meet, my role further evolved as a leader of worship, bringing the women to that place of quiet inner communion with the Spirit. We would sit in deep stillness and receive the love we needed to carry forth the mission that we felt Jesus was still entrusting to us.

Following Pentecost, we felt energized, renewed, and uplifted to begin some very important spiritual work for the planet. It did not dawn upon us how important this event was, but nevertheless, we began to secure the foundation of what later evolved into the church. Of course, we were still years away from a formalized institution.

My role as a leader of worship and communion solidified our ministry, and we grew as a body of believers. Even though we were believers in Jesus, the practice of our Jewish faith traditions also continued for a time. But more and more, through inner direction, we began to replace these traditional beliefs based on law and ritual.

Furthermore, after Jesus left, it was a time of great controversy. Many factors were at play in our culture that were not necessarily of a religious nature. People had to navigate through our troubled political and religious traditions, and there was chaos and social unrest. My life ended in a way that you would consider highly disturbing. But I met my death with faith and assurance of the eternal life Jesus promised. My leadership set a pattern for women who played an important role in the early Christian church, commonly known as "deaconesses."

As I close, I encourage you to allow the relationship bonds of Spirit to secure you in what you can achieve as a human. Life in the Spirit is the beautiful expression of the love in which we all exist as sons and daughters of God. May your spiritual life add more meaning and value to the world. Thank you, dear reader, and may my account touch your heart and uplift your soul.

"We are hoping to rectify the past and especially to end the male domination that has long persisted within the church."

6

MARY THE MAGDALENE

Greetings, this is Mary! You have come to know me as Mary the Magdalene or Mary Magdalene. Down through the ages, my name has come to refer to the iconic figure of "the fallen woman." And it is true that I did prostitute myself during a period when I believed I had no other options. Sadly, women all around the globe still face this very damaging plight.

The phrase "fallen woman" speaks to behavior deemed unacceptable and irresponsible and which religious traditions regard as sinful. And yet, I believed I was salvageable. Intuitively, I felt I was a good person, even if my culture told me I was condemned. When I first met him, the Master was able to look past all of this. He helped me sort through my predicament, and the sisters who rescued me did not make me feel dirty, ashamed, or guilty. In fact, their approach was very uplifting. They made me realize that if Jesus could see past my sins and still love and accept me, then I must be worthy of love. So I decided to leave my former occupation, follow the women, and engage with their growing ministry.

I have a message for men and women of your era who find themselves in a life of prostitution: You are absolutely worthy of something better. Your Indwelling Spirit has a divinely ordained plan for your life. Follow its leadings to reject this soul-crushing lifestyle. You have a right to be loved and nurtured by the Spirit! But when the conditions of your life have stripped away your sense of worth, and there seems to be no other choice than to sell your body, then it is time to take stock and ask for help. Most people do not know where or how to seek help. Plus, their feelings of unworthiness bring to bear so much pressure upon their psyche that they cannot hear the divine Inner Voice. But I say to you that you *can* hear it and there *is* help. And if my account can save even one person from this way of life then I am satisfied.

Returning to my story: My early upbringing was rather painful for me. I grew up in extreme poverty and there were other unfortunate occurrences that led me to work in a brothel. These are not easy words for me to speak because they underscore the despair I experienced when this seemed to be my only option—or so I thought at the time. My labors in the brothel are not worthy of recalling. Allow me to repeat my admonition to those who find themselves in a similar trap: Prostitution is a soul-deceiving way of life!

It was an auspicious day when two women from Jesus' Corps came into my place of employment in the town of Magdala. They spoke to me about the nature of the Spirit and the divine dignity that lives in every individual. When I heard these precious words, I knew this was the turning point in my life. They threw me a lifeline and I grabbed it with grateful hands.

I asked them to tell me more, so we entered into a long discussion on the loving nature of God and the immense value placed upon each person as an offspring of the Divine Source. That message alone was sufficient for me, so I immediately decided to leave the brothel with them. I felt trepidation because this was all so new to me and I did not really know these women. But at some level, I trusted them implicitly.

My first meeting with Jesus

When they introduced me to the Master, I fell apart completely and utterly. It was if everything in my life up to that point had suddenly collapsed. I was raw and exposed, but not in an embarrassing way. That's because the love Jesus poured into my heart gave me new life, stirring in me the hope that I was indeed worthy and salvageable. I felt as if the pieces of my psyche were being glued back together, but in a higher way!

Jesus knew I was broken in spirit and in body. He could see that in me, even though the women did not explicitly tell him what my profession had been. He just knew. He saw deep within me, and the understanding and compassion that flowed from him into my heart broke the spell of unworthiness. He uplifted me into a space where I was able to finally feel the dignity I knew was there but could not feel on my own. And this transformation happened because of the power of his love. Genuine love can work wonders when there is readiness to be healed and uplifted.

I was very fortunate to be in the immediate physical presence of Jesus. It is hard to put into words what it was like to be around this majestic personality. He saw me as a whole person. I was not a body to him, something to be used for pleasure. I was a living, breathing, thinking, feeling individual who had something worthy to contribute to life. Until then, I did not even know that was possible! Just being around him was enough to catalyze this change, once I had taken the faith-step of following my sisters in rejecting a life of sin. I was then ready to start a joyful life built on love and the sharing of that love in service to others.

I made the decision to follow the women into their life of service, but at first I did not know how I could best serve. I struggled with the question of what my real talents might be. It took time to become comfortable with my new way of life, and I still encountered prejudice regarding my former profession. Fortunately, the women who surrounded me were most gracious. They always helped me realize that their lack of judgment was truly what Jesus wanted all of us to experience. I learned that my own inner validation was enough to combat the disdain I sometimes felt from others.

Once I was fully invested in the power of my self-worth that Jesus had awakened in me, I began to live my life with new gusto and a heightened sense of purpose. I listened carefully to the discussions of the women and to Jesus' preaching whenever he was with us. I pondered his words carefully in my heart. And I marveled at the way he was able to illustrate truths from his parables that resonated with his followers.

I become chief speaker for the Women's Corps

Over time, I grew even more confident in my own abilities—I became bold in sharing my own thoughts and interpretations. It was so very heartening when someone responded to my ideas, filling me with joy and a sense of accomplishment. It eventually dawned on me that I was talented at speaking and teaching. When my sisters and I ventured forth into towns where we ministered to women, I found that my voice was heard and recognized.

As I gained more strength in my sense of self, I felt a power move through me, an energy that allowed me to teach those living truths that could touch a person in great need. My sisters recognized my natural ability, so they elected me to be the primary speaker for our group.

From this point forward, I made bold to speak truth to those individuals who came from the various towns, villages, and cities to hear us. These were people who wanted to learn of a better way—the life of the Spirit, the life of freedom.

As we entered various parts of Palestine, the women in these regions would come out to meet us. They were highly curious about our group of women attached to Jesus. And as our acclaim continued to grow, we were able to draw more and more people to our encampments for healing and spiritual ministry. These meeting places were never permanent; we always established a temporary space during our periods of travel, making it easier for us to receive and minister to the local people.

You might imagine that some women were shocked that a person such as I could receive salvation, start a new life, and become a public speaker and preacher. It was also very unusual in those days to encounter a group of women possessing full authority to speak on behalf of a man like Jesus.

In time, other women who started out like me followed us into the encampment and they, too, told their tales. With graciousness, we received them all. We never looked at them with judgment but rather with great pity and compassion. We all understood the tenuous position of females in our culture, how regimented women's roles were, and how there was no room for independent thinking or action outside of what was prescribed for us.

Jesus' reputation as a spiritual teacher and healer was by then creating a great "buzz" throughout the region of Palestine. We knew that spies had been sent by the Sanhedrin to take careful note of what Jesus was preaching and the healings that occurred within our midst. While this was very disconcerting to us, it did not seem to bother the Master. At least his outward demeanor was one of poise and cheerfulness, and he went about his various ministrations with an open heart that conveyed his great love and compassion.

How Jesus elevated women's status

Jesus elevated the position of women to equal status with men in a way that was revolutionary. Can you imagine our surprise and delight when we learned about an aspect of God that is nurturing and motherly? This idea was of course entirely new. Yet it made sense to us that Deity would have to be inclusive of the mothering nature that we embodied as women.

Unfortunately, this new concept was very troubling to the male apostles. This difficulty even extended to the spies who reported back to the Jewish authorities about how his teachings went against the grain of long-established traditions. Nevertheless, this message was extremely liberating and edifying for us women. And, as my other sisters have shared with you, this teaching undergirded the development of the social fabric that later evolved into the Christian church.

Wherever Jesus taught, women came to listen and the Women's Corps followed up with them. Because of this repeated exposure to new women, my voice became even more prominent. I spoke from the heart. I spoke from the depths of my soul about my experience, my life, and how Jesus liberated me from that path of sin and soul-destruction.

Unfortunately, my personal relationship with Jesus has become highly distorted throughout the ages. Jesus and I did not marry, as some of your false tales and fables promote. However, I did feel what you might call a soul marriage to him, as did my other sisters. There was an unbroken bond between us of a deep love that is very hard to define in human words. It was totally fulfilling even though it was not of a physical nature. It struck such deep chords within us that it even seemed *physically* satisfying. But it was so much more than even that. His love fostered the fulfillment of our self-identity. We were now beloved daughters of God. We knew we had a place in the Kingdom of Heaven or what you might call "the Family of Love."

When Jesus made bold to announce his oneness with God, it was not hard for us to fathom that profound truth. The majesty of his character and the way he conducted himself easily led credence to the fact that here was indeed God personified. Can you imagine how many of us sought to be in his presence? His love, that pure pristine affection emanating from his divine heart, was so soul-satisfying and so identity-enriching that we always, always sought to be around him.

How we loved him! You could call it a kind of adoration, but we also loved him because he gave us permission to be more than we thought we were—to find those deep places of potential and draw them out through loving service. And this is the way that eventually leads to life eternal.

The time of trial and the resurrection

All of a sudden, hard times came upon us. The Master began to speak more urgently of an impending crisis, about the plan for his destruction. It terrified us! It was unfathomable to think there could be people who wanted to harm this most beautiful person. But he was frank and he disclosed that his time among us would soon end. Yet he still encouraged us, even in the face of all this bad news: He informed us that he would supply something to replace him, but we had no idea what that could be. However, we trusted him implicitly. And when the time came that he gave up his human life, our hearts were made glad on the day of resurrection even though this event was at first highly mystifying.

Many of my sisters have shared their accounts about this time of trial between Good Friday and Easter Sunday. What follows is my own personal experience as I encountered the empty tomb and saw the Master in his resurrected body.

Early Easter morning, I decided to go to the tomb of Jesus, bringing along with me several of my sisters of the Corps and a few other women. We wanted to properly pre-pare Jesus' body for burial according to our custom. After he was crucified, his body had been hastily moved to the tomb in the garden of Joseph of Arimathea and we were very disturbed that the appropriate care had not been taken. The women who accompanied me were my Corps sisters Joanna and Susanna and two mothers of male apostles, Mary and Salome. As we walked toward the garden, we became very alarmed when we saw Roman soldiers run past us, so we approached the garden tomb with trepidation. To our great surprise, we found the door to the tomb open with the large boulder guarding its entrance moved to one side.

As I approached the grave and peered in to see nothing there, my heart was very heavy both with sorrow and disbelief. My emotions gave way and I screamed! After my initial shock abated, I wept profusely. And then, as if a light suddenly warmed my soul, I heard a voice. At first it was strange: it sounded so familiar, yet it was also very different. In a moment of revelation, it finally dawned upon me who it was! My strongest feeling was one of great joy. But I also wondered: "How is this possible? Is this real? Am I looking at an apparition?" The Master was truly standing before me, but he also looked different than before. Seeing him resonated deeply within me. I knew he was really there!

I exclaimed this news to my sisters, who were standing nearby, and they also came to him. And as we adjusted ourselves to his glorified presence and began to grasp what this meant, our hearts burst with joy. However, at first not fully understanding this miracle, some of the woman experienced feelings of disbelief.

We quickly set out to bring the great news to our brethren, the eleven who were in hiding. They did not respond well to our report, as you know from the gospel account. For you see, there was so much bias that it was hard for them to imagine that the Master would have approached us first. Our brothers did not trust our story, thinking we must be demented by grief. It took them a long time to appreciate the fact that we were the first ones the resurrected Jesus had encountered.

Was it a matter of chance that we went to the gravesite, or were we guided there? I believe we were guided there. There must have been some overarching plan to bring us to the tomb to witness what we did, to bear witness to the fact that he was indeed among us.

As a side note, we hold our brothers in deep respect for all they accomplished in their public ministry. And yet, even in your modern day, many women have to deal with a double standard because of male dominance. For us, it was far worse. Jesus had already done much to elevate us out of that terrible situation, and his previous support gave us enough strength to stand in the courage of our own experience of witnessing his resurrection.

Following Easter Sunday and his resurrection, we wondered what was next. Events soon unfolded to guide us. The most important of these, of course, was Pentecost, when he imparted his Spirit of Truth as his personal connection to us, conveyed through the Holy Spirit.

The Women's Corps after Pentecost

The ministry of Jesus had moved from town to town, and as I said, our encampments followed him as he travelled. So now we needed to determine how to continue without such camps. Some of us decided to follow the male apostles in their travels, joining their ranks despite the highly discouraging fact that schisms had arisen because of their individualistic interpretations of Jesus' teachings. In the face of that difficulty, these women felt they could improve the situation by becoming a unifying and socializing presence with these men as they travelled about.

Other women elected to stay in the immediate area of Jerusalem. There they could continue to provide a space of reception for those who were curious or hungry for upliftment and spiritual truth. While many still sought healing for their physical maladies, we always encouraged them to also seek the spiritual healing that Jesus had so magnificently promoted and taught us.

While the members of the Corps were spreading out geographically, our spiritual unity remained strong. We held fast to the loving relationships we had cultivated during our time with the Master. Nevertheless, there was still much confusion, even after the time of Pentecost. Because of the political turmoil, we had to be extremely careful in how we ministered to those who came to us with open minds and hearts.

There are very few records of what truly transpired during this pivotal time after Pentecost and before the more formalized institution of the Christian church. In particular, the myths about my life began early on to foster a certain mystique about me.

Confusion about my life and my role set in because I did not leave behind anything in writing. In recent times, a written text attributed to me, *The Gospel of Mary*, has been discovered. This fragment is actually the narration of another woman's story. And this story actually pales in comparison with our real achievements. Those who read the so-called *Gospel of Mary* will need to spend time in discernment with it. And yet, it matters not to me what a person believes about such things. It is more a matter of how you comport yourself with your brothers and sisters and whether you are maintaining an attitude of love and a desire to be of service to them.

The role of women in the socialization
of spiritual culture

At one point I also embarked upon a missionary journey, but only as part of a group of sisters. In the course of these travels, our socialization network expanded little by little. And by the time Paul became an apostle, the network of believers we had fostered was strong enough to make Paul's ministry possible.

Unfortunately, we detected a high degree of misogyny in his teachings and we did not have much influence with him to change his position on women's proper role. It is very unfortunate that in the later development of the Christian church, the role of women as leaders, teachers, preachers, and healers was denied to us, in large part because of Paul's influence.

But I digress here a bit and wish to return to the time when we were still ministering as best we could throughout a broad region. The Master's message of love and faith in the Father stayed with us. And it did provide fertile ground to bring more people to us who sought spiritual healing.

Over time, however, the influence of the Women's Corps waned. As it did, certain perspectives about Jesus' life began to supplant the gospel as we understood it, especially in regard to the social aspect of the community of believers in the loving message of Jesus. The women who engaged in this work of the socialization of the teachings of Jesus became so marginalized that we even began to feel that our work was almost for naught. What now exists is a religion that has crystallized various teachings: some from Jesus, some from the male apostles, and much more from the many centuries of interpretation.

What we want now to accomplish with this account is a return to the simple gospel of Jesus: Salvation is achieved through faith in God as our Creator Parent, along with the growth and socialization of the brotherhood and sisterhood of humanity. Once the world truly embraces this dynamic teaching, you will experience more peace and harmony in your social relationships and the seeds we planted will finally bear fruit.

As I end my story, let one additional thing be noted: We are hoping to rectify the past and especially end the male domination that has long persisted within the Christian church. The proper role of women in spiritual development is paramount to creating a balance between the realization of God as Father and God as Mother. This balance is part of the divine plan for each evolutionary world. The fact that the church has experienced so much male domination under-scores the need for a resurgence in the recognition of the mothering aspect of Deity. This is critical in order for your world to reach its destiny of heaven on earth—that is, as a planet settled in Light and Life, as *The Urantia Book* puts it.

Since many are unaware that each planet has a divine plan, let our account inspire people to understand the natural and organic role that women play in developing a socialized spiritual culture. How we lived our individual lives is not as important as the social dynamic we created within the encampments. What is most essential is the fact that our work as the Women's Corps set apart by Jesus was to disseminate this socializing and healing aspect of spiritual growth. We pursued this essential mission while the message of the gospel was being shared by the male apostles.

Finally, I wish to emphasize how important and auspicious is the timing now for believers to better appreciate the role of women in the development of a spiritualized social culture. A movement for a form of spiritual socialization inclusive of women's roles is gaining momentum and will become a major force in the restructuring of the socializing institutions of religion world-wide.

What we intend with this book is to provide a means for people to ponder what we did and to think about the central role we played. This may be very difficult and even controversial for many. But the seed must be planted, and we have carefully cultivated this seed over the long years of the evolution of the Christian church. Now the sprouts of its germination process have reached a point where the minds and hearts of many are ready to embrace this approach.

While I could go further into the record of how my life unfolded, I do not want that to detract from our message about the nature of our ministry. It is time for all people to step out of the stain of their own unworthiness. Now is the time to recognize their true status as beloved and valuable children of our Creator who are called to participate in the great evolutionary restructuring of spiritual consciousness on the planet.

My life was one of service and I am so grateful that I was able to find Jesus and to play the role I did in ministering in the gospel he taught us. While my time on earth was short, now on my higher ascension journey I look back with great fondness on the experiences I had.

Let our experiences speak to your hearts. Let the influence of the Holy Spirit, our Divine Mother, move mightily through these words to transport you into the presence of Jesus, so that his indwelling Spirit of Truth may communicate even more broadly and deeply to your heart and soul the majesty of what it means to be human. The glory Jesus portrayed of his humanity is something each individual can achieve. It is only a matter of desiring and devoting the resources of mind and heart to find the Father within and then making that relationship the utmost priority for your life.

What more can I say? One day when the full fruition of the gospel has embraced the entire planet, then we members of the Women's Corps will feel that our work has produced the fruits of our hearts' desire.

"His approach was so logical and refreshing that you
could only view it as the actual truth."

7

MILCHA

I was cousin to Thomas Didymus, one of Jesus' original apostles. Curiosity was the motive for much of his interest in the Master. Because of his highly skeptical and questioning mind, he struggled to reconcile his beliefs about Jesus with his actual relationship to him.

I was first introduced to the Master by listening to cousin Thomas as he shared reports of his experiences as part of Jesus' preaching ministry. I became fascinated by what he told us about the gospel of the Kingdom of Heaven within. The idea that something perfect was seated within my being was quite compelling and intriguing. This concept spoke to a certain idealism within me, something that I had not been able to cultivate. To me, this ideal seemed both unattainable and unrealistic because of cultural assumptions about our roles as women.

I began to hear more about Jesus, and when an opportunity opened for me to come before this august person, I could actually feel the magnitude of his love emanating from his being. As with my other sisters, simply being with him changed me in ways I could barely understand at that time.

My cousin Thomas was the great influence that led me to Jesus. Thomas taught me a set of principles for evaluating truth based on the Master's teachings that helped me accept the validity of the gospel. That is not to say that my cousin and I discerned truth in the same way. Because he was male, Thomas had developed a more materialistic viewpoint than I that biased his outlook. This was a strong thread in him because of the way he was raised. He was heavily influenced by Jewish culture, which was highly prized within our family. I, too, was trained in these traditional religious tenets and precepts, but there was also a dormant feeling that would surface from time to time that encouraged me to open to a different way of looking at life.

How and why I decided to follow Jesus

When I first met Jesus, this latent capacity came alive in my heart and mind. Thanks to further conversations with my cousin and with women who followed Jesus, I soon struck out on my own and began to follow him.

I became involved during Jesus' early public ministry. I observed that some people listened while others were skeptical or even very doubtful and disdainful. But for me, it was a time of inner development as I posed questions within my mind and heart about the nature of reality and Jesus' exhortation to look within to find the Kingdom of Heaven. My interest in Jesus continued to grow because of several factors I will share below.

First, he elevated the greatest truths to be found within the Jewish tradition and brought them to life in a very practical manner. To me, his sublime interpretations represented the highest caliber of spiritual insight and wisdom. These teachings fed that part of me that had been conditioned by the way women were treated. He exalted concepts within the Jewish tradition that were inclusive of both genders, thus helping the women of our day appreciate their divine dignity. His approach was so logical and refreshing that you could only view it as the actual truth.

For many men, his advocacy for equality was very difficult to accept. They could not reconcile this teaching with their traditions. But for me, these ideas were liberating! I began to see the practicality in what he taught about our Heavenly Parent being accessible to all regardless of what we looked like on the outside or the differences we held within.

The second thing that attracted me to Jesus was the consistency in his teachings. You could not sense anything false within them. What he taught was truth—pure truth.

A third aspect of my growing attachment to the Master was his constancy in dealing with people. He was so even-handed. He rarely lost his composure, and the only time I ever saw what might be called mild impatience was when he rebuked a certain individual. But even this rebuke was done with such love and compassion that this person could hardly take offense.

My journey into the deeper meanings of the gospel

Much of what we perceive in a personal relationship is not through the senses of sight and hearing. Rather, it is through an emotional sensibility to how words are conveyed. When Jesus spoke, he was always so gracious, inviting, and welcoming. It was as if he was speaking another language—a language of the heart that was so engaging and attractive. Even when dealing with his enemies, he did not strive with them. He held his own with them in order to elevate these people to the higher truths he so magnificently taught.

Most of my sisters related to him through this more heartful approach. I did as well, but he also mightily appealed to my mind—my intellectual capacity. Perhaps because of my family background, I became heavily engaged with the intellectual comprehension of his religious tenets. So, when Jesus spoke, it resonated deeply within my mind even as I also felt my emotions stir. Because I enjoyed both levels of comprehension, I experienced a wonderful time of growth as so many false beliefs and ideologies began to fall away.

I became increasingly able to help the women understand his higher teachings. I explained his ideas from a different standpoint than the men. Sometimes my sisters would come to me with a question Jesus had posed, asking me how to answer and interpret it. Then we would sit together for a discussion.

Doing so was very valuable to us as women because we were not allowed to share our ideas with men due to their lack of respect for us. Instead of going to the men, we women had many discussions among ourselves about Jesus' teachings as we sat together in prayerful contemplation of the deeper aspects of spiritual growth.

All this became possible because Jesus was a master communicator. He took time with people and was inordinately patient in allowing them to share what was on their hearts and minds. When it was my turn to come before him and simply sit with him, something stirred within me because of the way he was present to me and allowed me to speak. I then felt the love Jesus stimulated within me bubble up to the surface of my being. My Spirit later helped me perceive the higher meaning of his approach, and I soon felt very empowered by it. My encounters with Jesus caused the limitations of my culture to recede; my strong attachment to the past increasingly diminished. The ultimate effect was to solidify an inner knowing that I had a role to play in his ministry and in supporting the gospel he so patiently and creatively taught us.

At first, I did not know what my role would be. I was fine with slowly discovering my purpose as I listened more closely to his parables and the deep truths he taught. But over time, and along with those around me, it was if a collective light turned on inside us.

Some people had very profound openings and awakenings of Spirit. For me, it was more gradual. Ideas would form in my mind of a higher order that created within me such lightness of being and joy in my heart. As these concepts developed, the radiating effect upon my emotions was very uplifting. I began to let go of the disdain from some of my male compatriots who did not understand the role of women in society, even though Jesus had elevated us to a higher position.

What more can I say? You, too, have the opportunity to experience these things for yourself. Even though he is not physically present with you, access to him now is even more pervasive through his Spirit of Truth. Every person has direct personal access to him should they desire to open this inner door to experience Jesus very intimately and lovingly.

The complex social environment around Jesus

All these experiences led me to join the ministering corps. We were a very diverse group of women coming from different backgrounds and family situations. Most of us had Jewish tradition as a common factor in our backgrounds. But this was secondary to our being united through our love for Jesus and our desire to assist him in his healing mission.

We had to maneuver amidst the varied opinions of people regarding Jesus as well as our own work as women. We witnessed how Jesus was hounded by an array of people who only wanted to stifle him. In addition, we ourselves often encountered a particular type of disdain. Sadly, this kind of discrimination is still rampant among some present-day social groups.

We also had to handle the simplistic and superstitious mindset of many of the common people. As a result, some came looking for miracles—for a spontaneous change that made their lives easier and less painful. While some of this attitude still exists in your culture, it was pervasive in my day. To discourage such "wonder-seeking," Jesus put the onus of responsibility on each person whenever he portrayed the higher truths of cosmic reality. The Women's Corps had many discussions about his approach to such issues, taking each teaching apart and putting it into the more familiar context of our own life experiences. Since I was more or less trained to be a critical or analytical thinker, I was also able to handle his statements through a rational, logical, and methodical process, while most of my sisters related to him more through intuition. These differences allowed us to have many edifying discussions whose aim was to flesh out the bigger picture presented in his teachings.

The added element that helped us in our truth discernment was, of course, what we experienced when we were in proximity to the radiance of his love and compassion. It was so palpable that it seemed to cement into our minds and bodies a higher reality of living truth.

The encampment was a place of diverse activities. Jesus had created a tremendous amount of interest in himself and many, many individuals poured in to see him. Some came to hear and meet him from the highest and purest of motives, but the majority were purely curiosity seekers. And as I said, there were others who attempted to foster dissension among the loyal ranks.

Our faith in Jesus and the truths he taught infused our methods for handling the encampment environment. We were able to provide a stabilizing influence because we ministered to the needs of the body as well as the needs of the soul. The synergy of our combined feminine qualities provided a foundation of security—a bastion where people could go and be in a place of peace that temporarily provided a departure from the chaos of the world. We fortified people through our ministrations of the heart, soul, and body and gave them an opportunity to relax and find distance from their troubled lives.

Our methods were different from how the male apostles preached and organized their ministry to the multitudes in the encampment. Their approach could sometimes cause conflict because they would contrast the beliefs of individuals with Jesus' teachings. At times, the apostles had difficulty translating the higher meanings of what Jesus taught. On the other hand, we women operated in a different emotional environment.

We were more concerned with the healing process and all that comes from taking a person in great pain—physical, emotional, or mental—and helping them find solace and comfort. We differed in our approach to ministry from our brothers because of our relationship with Jesus, who helped us see the deepest needs within a person.

The women learn to minister from the Spirit

I will now share what occurred within the encampment during the period after Jesus formally commissioned us as the Women's Evangelistic Corps.

We divided our efforts into teams as did the male apostles. For example, some sisters procured funds and supplies for us, some took on the responsibility of ministering to the children, and others were more inclined to minister to the physical needs of those who came to us.

The major and common thread was that we were all gaining strength and skill in ministering from the Spirit. We learned to love and appreciate people exactly as they were. We regarded each soul as precious—a soul encased within a physical body that was undergoing mental, emotional, and physical stress, thus leading to a wide range of ailments and illnesses.

We knew that many did not come to us for spiritual upliftment. They simply needed help, various kinds of support, most often for the needs of their bodies. To us, the spiritual needs of their souls were more essential than their physical needs, so we ministered to them in Spirit at the same time that we attended to their physical problems. At all times, we shared the pearls of wisdom that Jesus had taught us.

When people asked questions about the teachings, we followed the Master's example of feeling into their deepest needs and speaking to their innermost longings. We learned that this type of engagement plants a kernel of truth within them that later expands to enlighten their minds.

We began to witness how many people we ministered to became more inclined to love and forgive one another. This allowed them to put aside petty grievances and differences so they could more firmly grasp the truths of the gospel of the Parenthood of God as the unifying factor that made possible a positive and healthy familial bond. The male apostles were not as equipped for this style of ministration because we had been the nurturers for our own families and also because we were expressing out innate feminine nature. But none of this is to say that these men did not do their best.

How the Women's Corps seeded the growth of the early church

I recall vividly what occurred in the encampments after we were well-established in our ministry. The women would convene each evening to discuss the affairs of the day. We communed with one another and with the Spirit and developed more sisterly compassion and understanding for one another. I cannot say for sure whether this occurred with the men. But after sundown, they also spent time together in their own way, sitting around the campfire, talking and sharing.

Prior to the time of Jesus' arrest and crucifixion, the cohesiveness of our women's group had increased even further. Perhaps in anticipation of what was to come, we had knit together our relationship into a very strong container that held us together even during his death and resurrection. Our group solidarity might well be considered the seed of the Christian church, but this cohesion was not founded on holding certain beliefs.

Yes, it is true that what the apostles preached after the resurrection did inspire many people, but this was not the foundation of the movement. The true foundation was *spiritual*. From a modern-day standpoint, you might call it "energetic." And this is a spiritual principle that the Christian church still needs to understand over 2,000 years later. The real foundation of the church is a form of kinship, a recognition that we are all members of a loving divine family operating in an evolutionary continuum under the Parenthood of our Holy Creator.

So much of what is passed down as truth in Christian theology is merely opinion based upon interpretations. Also, there has been a dynamic of antagonism and jockeying for position as to whose belief is superior or more accurate. But this way of proceeding interferes with the underlying spiritual kinship, diminishing it and making it less operative. Despite these difficulties, the fundamentals and the foundations of spiritual connection we experienced long ago are still available today—even as the church outworks many years of theological deviation from the truth of the message of Jesus and the simple gospel he preached.

Today there are winds of change within the church regarding women. A growing vibrancy of spiritual energy is opening the females of your world to a greater expansion and expression of Jesus' presence within them. My sisters and I have long anticipated this opportunity for the world's consciousness to change. Sharing our story will help many of our dear sisters come into their power as daughters of God, awakened to the Spirit within.

Our story represents the genesis of the Christian church, but we had no idea we were birthing a social institution. Instead, we thought we were growing a family that cared for one another in an effort to find collective solutions that would uplift all at the same time. Our growth came from continuing to build upon this familial relationship, and we were highly successful to the point that the teachings began to spread, drawing more people into the spiritual synergy of the growing community.

And we now know there was another factor. Jesus traveled throughout the Middle East and the Roman Empire prior to his public ministry in an effort to prepare people around the Mediterranean world to receive his message of love. He planted seeds for others to receive our family energies as these energies traveled to those remote places to feed those souls. This is something we became aware of during our afterlife journeys.

And this same dynamic is so necessary again now—to build the family of love as a planet-wide culture which will enable the living gospel of Jesus as he originally taught it to come back to full life, full force, full vitality, and stir the hearts of all. Jesus' universal Spirit of Truth is well able to catalyze this growing planetary phenomenon of Christ consciousness.

As I end my account, please consider these closing thoughts: Open more fully to Jesus so that he may share with you his life experience as a human. Let his wisdom guide you as you traverse your own internal changes. Whether you are aware of it or not, you are on a path of self-awareness that leads to self-mastery. Let Jesus' mastery of his human life guide you now. Let his presence steer you out of all that causes you consternation, all that frustrates you, all that even angers you at times because of what your culture is now undergoing. Let him be your anchor. There is something so beautiful, so true, so humanly divine when you come close to Jesus in this way. If it feels right, simply sit with this idea now and allow yourself to experience intimacy with Jesus. Welcome these times of change, knowing he is with you. Know that you are guided and loved beyond measure —and that with him and in him, all is well.

"When he ministered to a person, Jesus could intuit
which healing natural substance they needed, and he
also invoked the power of the Holy Spirit
into this medicine."

8

NASANTA

My name is Nasanta. It is my pleasure to share my life experiences as you continue to explore the rich dimensions of our sacred work as ministers of the gospel of Jesus.

To introduce myself, I'll begin with my family. My father was a physician. Alleviating human suffering was his great passion, and some of that zeal must have rubbed off on me. As I was growing up, he recognized my interest in his work and began to teach me about the nature of various ailments. He also shared what he used as agents to support the healing process. My mother was also involved in our family business, as she prepared many of the unguents, potions, and other medicines or techniques that we used in healing. In fact, our home environment was very regimented due to my helping my mother in the preparations of these healing substances. In addition to all that, my father also believed in a metaphysical aspect to healing. For example, he recited incantations for the sake of his patients that he thought had magical properties.

I was not raised in the Jewish religious tradition as were most of the other women in the Corps. My family studied the workings of the natural physical world, plus I shared my father's strong interest in metaphysics.

As I matured, my father brought me on board in the role of an assistant, so I learned from him by directly observing how he attended to his patients. Over time, I began to feel something rumble within me that led me to explore the rich vein of knowledge that constitutes true healing.

My first meeting with Jesus activates my healing vocation

I first encountered Jesus during one of his public visits to our area. His fame preceded him as a teacher and healer. My curiosity was piqued, so my family and I went to hear him with his apostles in attendance. Prior to first seeing Jesus, my inner "rumblings" had become even more prominent. Something new was moving in me, something that I could feel but also found mystifying. When I listened to Jesus, this deep feeling connected with his words, as if they went right into me. He spoke a language that soothed these rumblings but was somehow activating and uplifting at the same time.

I made bold to go before him and seek his blessing. He laid his hands upon my head, and I immediately felt energy shoot through his hands, move downward, and spark in my heart something I did not even know was there! To this very day, even here in my heavenly abode, I can clearly recall this experience because it was the catalyzing moment of truth I had been searching for as a young woman. As this sacred energy from his hands entered my heart, a voice within me said, "This is your calling and purpose. Will you answer the call?" The voice was so strong that I simply *had* to answer "Yes!" to this mission of alleviating human suffering. And I intuitively knew my healing work would address physical ailments as well as that painful type of suffering that comes from feeling lost, alone, and abandoned.

Initially, I was unsure about approaching Jesus to volunteer for his gospel work. Part of my uncertainty had to do with my personal prejudice about Jesus being from the Jewish religious tradition; this bias even impacted my ability to understand him intellectually, even though at a soul level I knew his love was beginning to speak to a deep inner yearning. I did not realize at first how open he was to all humanity regardless of a person's gender, belief system, or role in society. He was truly the most magnanimous individual I have ever known! Because of this, I misunderstood him due my *own* lack of magnanimity. Nevertheless, he had catalyzed something so strong that I could not deny its presence.

I continued to apply myself to my father's work with a goal of learning more about his profession, though my presence as a woman was not always welcome. My father did not dissuade me from my interests, but he truly did not understand what was in my heart. As I learned new skills, I became more proficient in recognizing disease symptomology and determining what natural healing substances were helpful in relieving symptoms. But something was still pressing upon my heart—certain dreams and desires Jesus had activated.

When the disciples of Jesus returned to my area, I visited with them to learn more about Jesus' ministry and especially to find out about his miraculous healings. I was soon introduced to the devoted and dedicated women in the encampment.

I could see right away that Jesus' female followers were ardent; they displayed a great affection for the Master and were loyally following him. I entered into a deep conversation with one of them and was mightily influenced by her experience with Jesus. As she spoke of his sincerity and his utterly loving manner toward each individual, I began to realize how rare this man was.

I continued these discussions and visited the encampments when I could. I spent the most time with the women, sharing with them my interest in healing and my training experiences under my father. Before long, they invited me to join their group, but I was unsure at first. I felt like an outsider because I did not share their Jewish beliefs. I was a bit standoffish for a time, but something kept drawing me back to them.

My life-changing second encounter with Jesus

At one point, however, I had a new opportunity to directly speak with Jesus. In this second encounter, I had yet another profound experience with him, even more so than the first time when he blessed me with his hands.

He was direct in approaching me, but did so in a very humble and unassuming way. There was an unmistakable aura of goodness around him, and the kinship bond I felt with him was almost immediate. I could sense his sincerity, kindness, compassion, and his keen interest in who I was and why I was interested in his ministry. His love of humanity spoke volumes to my heart, as if lifting me into a wide, deep, and elevated awareness of the goodness in which he lived.

As I experienced these things, I suddenly made a decision that changed my life. I now understood what the other women had experienced around him! All I can say is that his goodness was so compelling that I simply wanted and needed to be around it. It was pure. It was sweet. It was simple. But this feeling was also strong and commanding. Being in his presence was unlike anything I had ever known before.

I asked if I could spend more time with the women to learn from them and of course to have more encounters with Jesus. They accepted me willingly, even though I was a gentile. You might consider this as not-so-significant in your day, but in my time it was very unusual.

I decide to join the Women's Corps as a healer

Now, I still had some lingering thoughts arising from what you might call divided loyalties, so I shared that concern with Jesus. He helped me recognize the higher calling of the Spirit within more clearly and pointed out that my first duty was to God. But in no way, he said, was any of this said in disrespect to my father, his profession, or my family life. Jesus helped me see how I could serve God and still retain my status as a dutiful daughter, even while demonstrating a greater expression of love for my family than before.

With this understanding, I went to visit my family along with some of the women of the encampment. These sisters strongly supported me as I asked my father for his permission to join their group, the special corps of women who were devoting their lives to ministering in the gospel of Jesus.

At first my father expressed reservations. He said that my request was both highly irregular and also went against the grain of his beliefs. But he also could clearly see how I was turning into a healer of a different sort, and his higher nature prevailed as he gave me permission to join their ranks and seek my own path. I sensed that he knew I had real skill and promise as a healer and did not wish to prevent me from my heart's desire. Of course, it was unusual in our culture to allow a woman to strike out on her own. So I honor my father for his courage in stepping outside the confines of tradition and allowing himself to be guided by his love for me and his desire for my happiness to prevail.

Upon receiving his permission and my family's blessing, I became a committed member of the women's encampment. I met this challenge with great hope in my heart and yet with mental trepidation about my lack of understanding of the nature of the women's work with Jesus. But that concern was soon allayed when they began to teach me about the role of faith and the power of living in the Spirit.

As I became more invested in the teachings and closely observed the women's daily ministry, my inner desire to be a healer deepened into a remarkable new awareness.

I could then tap into a profound power I previously did not know existed. This change was especially catalyzed when, in the encampments, I was confronted with so much human suffering and poverty of awareness, which Jesus sometimes called "the poverty of the spirit." As I was drawn into deeper love and compassion for these people in need, my calling to be a healer seemed to spring to new life, and this expanded sense of mission became "married" to the medical knowledge I had acquired from my father. I soon found myself teaching my sisters about the medicinal properties of healing herbs, unguents, and ointments. When these methods were combined with the love we all felt for our needy brothers and sisters, the people we ministered to had mighty healing responses.

As time went on, I increasingly deepened my grasp of faith. I gained a better comprehension of the goodness of our Creator and of the corresponding desire within the human heart to become more Godlike. These were the teachings Jesus so generously and magnanimously shared with us. He understood how disconnected people were from God and knew how to bring them back to a life of faith.

What Jesus revealed to us about the healing process

Jesus knew what was needed for genuine healing. He lived it, applied it, and instructed us about what constitutes true healing. I use the phrase "true healing" because the essence of healing comes from the Spirit. When the Spirit is invoked, it forms a foundation upon which the energies of the body and mind can align. Jesus explained this process in terms of the action of the Holy Spirit as a mothering essence that is able to restructure a living organism to conform to divine patterns and principles.

Because of his superb awareness of the Holy Mother Spirit, Jesus taught special things to us as his female apostles—even as he pursued a different approach with his male apostles, his disciples, and his other followers. When he spoke to us about the motherly aspect of the Holy Spirit, he reinforced our understanding that women are by nature the containers of life. Because we have an innate capacity to express our Divine Mother's gift of life and well-being, he instructed us in this aspect of feminine Deity and explained to us how the Holy Spirit engages in healing.

Many of us had been trained in the use of remedies that had been handed down from our mothers and grandmothers. And as I shared earlier, I had trained under my father, who was a healing professional. So, we as a group had a fairly broad knowledge of the gifts of the natural world to heal and sustain human life. Jesus well understood this aspect of the work, but he taught us about the additional component of the Holy Spirit's action, which added to the efficacy of the healing substances we used.

When he ministered to a person, Jesus could intuit which healing natural substance they needed. He then invoked the power of the Holy Spirit into the medicine, which in turn energized it to create a more efficacious response. Jesus' love and compassion also infused power into the healing substance.

Our ministry spread widely, especially after Jesus left us, because we were at that time imbued with the power of his Spirit of Truth. We continued our supplications to the Divine Mother, for her action as the Holy Spirit to move its energies into our medicines. Many people we treated had been conditioned to believe that illness was a sign of God's disfavor, creating a mighty mental impediment to their getting well. But when they were in our encampment and surrounded by its pervasive aura of love, they started to soften and open their minds to receive our gifts of healing.

We continued to meet with success, but many of the male apostles were mystified by our healing work. Jesus had instructed them about the healing process, but it was difficult for them to understand this because of their different mentality. They had witnessed many healings at Jesus' hands and ours, so they left most of the healing to us and went about their preaching and teaching as best as they knew.

During our time, there were many cults devoted to the worship of "the goddess." Jesus helped me understand that these religious expressions were actually a human representation of the Divine Mother in whom all life exists. He helped me appreciate that I had direct access to this Deity Person and that, as my Mother, she wanted me to grow in my awareness of her presence. With this improved understanding, I applied myself even more diligently to commune with her. I set time aside each day to sit and ask her to show me who she is. In fact, other sisters did this as well and we compared our experiences. We were learning that life in the body is beautiful and good, and that by appealing to Divine Mother, along with invoking the blessing of her presence in the medicines, many wonderful things could happen.

Finally, my direct training by Jesus also produced many "fruits of the spirit" in my life. The most important was compassion for human nature and all of its frailties. When I was around such a majestic person as Jesus, it was easy to see what an individual could achieve when totally dedicated to God's will. I now knew that this potential was real, but I also saw that it greatly contrasted with ordinary human frailty and suffering. While I marveled at Jesus' total devotion, I also witnessed his understanding that many individuals were simply unable to appreciate the true nature of our Creator's love.

Persecution disperses the women, but we meet again on high

My other sisters have related their sorrowful feelings during the period between the crucifixion and resurrection and I certainly felt those sentiments. However, our joy could barely be contained when we discovered that Jesus was still alive, albeit in a different form. The event of Pentecost that soon followed greatly uplifted my resolve to carry on my healing ministry and continue working with the Women's Corps. Fortunately, we were still able to procure funds and provisions from those who supported our ministry. I continued to focus on ministering to the healing of body and mind, but did not do as much teaching of the gospel as others did. I found great delight in my growing skill at being a practitioner of the healing arts who invoked the power of the Holy Spirit into my work.

The political unrest after the time of Pentecost became a serious factor affecting our healing and preaching ministry. We continued to be subjected to ridicule and derision by the Jewish authorities who were still trying to obscure the achievements of Jesus. It certainly was not an easy time for us. We banded together and grew a support system with the help of other believers and those who had also benefitted from our healing ministrations. You have heard from other sisters about how we built a foundation that later developed into the Christian church. It is not as important for me to discuss that fact as it is for me to inform you that I was sorely tested in my faith because of the way Jesus' followers were derided by our enemies.

I persevered through these actions directed against us. I did not feel that my life was in serious danger, so I simply ignored the ridicule because I believed so strongly in my work and the love Jesus had activated within me. Those women who stayed with the encampment felt the same way, and we grew even stronger as ministers, especially through group prayer and communion with the Spirit.

I never married. I elected to devote the rest of my life to serving my brothers and sisters through my skill and talent. This was a free-will choice from my heart because of my devotion to Jesus; it was almost impossible for me to fathom that I could do anything else. I poured my love into each individual, and you cannot imagine the joy I experienced when I saw the light of spiritual recognition turn on in a person's eyes. And even though conditions around us continued to escalate to the point of much chaos and dissension, we continued to persevere until we could no longer continue and remain safe.

We went into hiding for a time, then returned to our ministrations. But unfortunately, the persecutions started up again, this time more in earnest. My sisters bade me go back to my family for the sake of my safety, and it was with a heavy heart that I left them. So, I departed and I returned to my family, who welcomed me home. I picked up my medical work with my father, and continued to be a harbinger of truth to those who might be ready to hear the gospel of Jesus.

I had what you might call a rather long life in terms of the average life span of that time. When I gave up my life, I did so with a glad heart and walked into the embrace of Jesus, who was waiting for me. My sisters who experienced a more tumultuous end also walked into the arms of Jesus. Our reunion on the other side was an occasion of great joy as we shared our stories and then continued on our journey.

Dear ones, I'll end here so you can hear another's story. May you continue to comprehend Jesus' love of women, the empowerment he gave us to be true to ourselves, our gender, and what we offer our brothers and sisters in spiritual ministry.

"When Jesus revealed to us the reality of our
Divine Mother, can you imagine how liberating
and enlightening this was for us to hear?

9

RACHEL

My name is Rachel, and I was peripherally related to the Master as the sister-in-law of his brother in the flesh, Jude. I became aware of Jesus through the marriage of my sister to the Master's brother.

I knew Jude before Jesus began his public ministry because of Jude's marriage to my sister. Jude was a firebrand in temperament when he was young, sometimes getting in trouble with the Roman authorities because of his loose association with the Zealots.[4] But after he fell in love with my sister, his temperament began to mature. Jude realized he had to be a provider for her and present some form of stability to my father in order for him to grant permission to marry her.

Jude often shared stories with our family about his strange elder brother, especially about how Jesus had acted as a father

---

4 The young Jude was once imprisoned briefly by the Romans, but Jesus obtained his early release. This story is told at 126:8.3 in *The Urantia Book*.

to Jude and his siblings after Joseph died. Upon hearing this, I became intrigued by Jesus' unique methods of family management. I had never heard of such techniques before.

It was clear to me that Jude was highly impressed with his brother. He did not know what to make of him, but Jude certainly felt the magnitude of Jesus' personality. Yet, there was also a sense in which my brother-in-law was not able to fully appreciate the Master, because Jude had grown up with a child's perspective on him instead of being on equal par with Jesus as a peer.[5]

I soon began to hear more about Jesus from the gossip of the surrounding communities where he preached the living gospel of truth. I finally encountered Jesus on one of these preaching tours that brought him to Nazareth, where we lived. I immediately felt something stir within my soul and speak to my heart. I felt a deep hunger for more of the spiritual vitality that he so lavishly bestowed upon all who could receive his words of truth. I was mightily impressed by his demeanor—his composure, kindness, and graciousness. This man began to make a very profound mark on me, and I soon realized there was something quite special about him. At first, I was discouraged by some family members who thought Jesus was "way out of sorts." But nothing could dissuade me. Instead, I sensed an even deeper yearning to investigate what this unique person had to say and who he was. Later I learned that my other sisters of the yet-to-form Women's Corps had similar experiences after their own initial meetings with him.

Keep in mind that women of our day were not encouraged to have their own opinions. We were controlled by our

5 For details see *The Urantia Book*, 127:4.3.

male-dominated culture and the religious traditions that regulated the role of women in society. One thing remarkable to me was that Jesus encouraged us women to have our own views on things and to value our own thoughts. He gave us permission to examine and share our thoughts and feelings in contrast to what we had learned through our cultural and religious influences.

I decide to devote myself to Jesus

I then fell into a period of introspection. I could sense two influences pulling at me. On one hand, the teachings of Jesus resonated in my soul. But on the other, I felt the cultural pull of my tradition and the influences of the men in my life. It took time to sort this out, but before long the spiritual pull toward Jesus became predominant, and I was able to let go of traditional ideas that I soon saw as erroneous. I decided to investigate to my heart's satisfaction what Jesus taught and who he was. I also spoke with other women who were likewise inspired by Jesus' teachings.

By this time, Jesus had stirred up something profound throughout the region. It was as if our collective souls were being enlightened and enlivened. He had the whole area of Palestine very much agitated because he was speaking truths that struck against our ancient teachings. Some people were even knocked off balance by his ideas. For a time, he created quite a topsy-turvy situation in the hearts of many, especially those who had prejudices against him because he was a Galilean.

In spite of these difficulties, I sought out the women who were resonating with his gospel, and they welcomed me into their discussion groups. At first, they were not formally organized. What I found instead was simply a place where we women could share our opinions and not be judged or evaluated by our male cohorts. These early discussions and our ongoing encounters with Jesus eventually inspired me to devote all my time to supporting the gospel message.

As I said, this was a time of spiritual quickening, and real excitement percolated all around me. It was a time of mighty growth, profound searching, and inner seeking. I recall this period as one of the greatest experiences in my life. Even now, at the elevated level of my ascension career two millennia later, I can fondly look back at how much growth I achieved during this time.

Of course, at first we did not know that Jesus was the Creator of our universe; we did not understand who he truly was. But in looking back, I recall how thrilling it was to be in proximity to such a great one. Never before had this occurred in the world, and never again will it be thus. This was a unique moment! I now consider myself very fortunate to have been able to experience him not only in his humanity, but also to feel the divine essence he shared so freely and majestically with all who could resonate with him.

What drew us to him—what drew me to him—was love, pure and simple! The magnitude of his energy was palpable. It was a visceral experience. It is hard to describe what this was like. However, if you go within and ask for his presence to pervade you, your emotions can expand to feel the majestic love we also experienced.

How I became part of the Women's Corps

Eventually, I was introduced to the women who were firmly established in the encampment and who were devoted to following Jesus at all costs. These leaders invited me to investigate what they were doing—their healing and teaching work, and their unique process of coming into their own power as a group that Jesus supported. And these women were so open and welcoming to me.

At first, I received extra attention because I was the sister-in-law of the Master's brother. But that quickly wore off as I became more invested in the group's dynamics. I discovered that the women operated on an even playing field—no one was considered greater than anyone else because of their relationship with Jesus. Thanks to this atmosphere of equality, we began to explore the gifts each of us brought to the table.

We learned from one another, and as our other sisters have related, we shared freely. It was a time of "no holds barred." We felt safe. We felt secure, and more than that, we felt loved. This helped us put aside our egos and gain even more harmonious unity, even though we did not yet understand what we were birthing within our group.

Allow me to say more about my attraction to Jesus. Mind you, he was a very strong physical being. He was virile, and he radiated a type of male attractiveness that was very beautiful to behold. His countenance was peaceful, his demeanor serene. He bore himself like a king, and all of us sensed that a certain regality seemed to radiate from his being. I was drawn to him in a physical way, but it was not what you would call sexual. Rather, it was my appreciation for the beauty he exuded that was so compelling to be around.

His emotional disposition led him to convey deep compassion and understanding for the human condition. I resonated with this because I too was very moved and touched by people's suffering—their poverty and their illnesses. Jesus' compassion for them touched me deeply. I saw how he moved people, how he stirred that inner dimension of the Spirit to help them heal at a fundamental level.

I was mightily moved because he empowered us to follow his example. We were in very close proximity to him as he worked in the encampment, assisting him as he went around to each person to extend exhortations of cheerfulness and positivity, and encouraging them to find that inner strength and peace that arose from the spiritual quickening he evoked in people from all walks of life.

Lessons from Jesus applicable for modern healers

I recall one incident when he was ministering to a woman who was traumatized by some very debilitating illnesses. He bade me to come close to observe what he was doing and participate in the healing he was delivering. I sensed a "drawing in" movement toward this woman who was suffering so greatly. He first helped her find a place of inner quiet, and then he reached in even deeper to evoke a great change in her. I never forgot this, and this experience empowered me to open more fully to my own inner healing potential and, through deep compassion, I began to lead individuals into a more receptive and peaceful place to experience healing.

Sadly, what our Women's Corps accomplished is missing in your culture. By this I mean the very human yet divinely inspired healing touch that we learned about from Jesus.

When most people present with illness in your modern culture, they receive a diagnosis and then a certain medicine is prescribed to evoke a healing response or cure. We see this as a deficiency in your approach to medicine because it removes the very human healing touch that comes from empathizing with what that person is undergoing. An ill person—regardless of whether their condition is physical, mental, or emotional—needs to feel compassion. This is what Jesus dispensed so freely and generously. He understood what people were experiencing. It was as if he was right there with them, and that degree of presence did much to alleviate a person's suffering because now there was someone sharing that burden. It is a truism that when our burdens are shared, they become lighter.

That is not to say that we need to *carry* another's burden. Jesus taught us not to retain or hold on to a person's load of suffering, but instead to turn our healing work into the joyful experience of helping people gain a deeper understanding of their difficulties. How valuable were these lessons! How fundamental they were to our expanding interest in his healing ministry.

Of course, we did not understand very much at first. All we knew was that so many people were resonating with him. They were being uplifted, and something joyful began to percolate within them. This was not always because their illnesses were cured, but because they were being validated as worthy sons and daughters of God. Jesus always did that no matter who it was, no matter whether they believed in him or not. He was always willing to touch that deep inner place. Again, I say, this kind of intimacy in healing is missing from your culture.

To each person reading this account, I encourage you to sit with these ideas. Take a few moments to ask Jesus how he was able to find that depth within every person and how he transmitted healing energy into them.

Allow me to speak a further word of wisdom to those who practice healing in your modern-day culture: Find your compassion for those who come to you. If you cannot, then appeal to the Master and ask him to share his compassion with you, which you can then pass on to your patients. People need to feel this deep compassion and validation.

This kind of love cannot be manufactured in pill form. It must be experienced in a heart-to-heart setting, in a soul-to-soul experience of one human simply loving and appreciating another.

While these words may sound simple, we believe you have departed far from this more personal approach. It may not be easy to return to this place, although we do see a growing willingness to change. We wish to give you an empowering message that everyone can be a healer of others and everyone can heal themselves from within. I do not mean any of this as a criticism, but merely as an observation along with the hope that my words will stimulate a widespread call to action.

Now, of course, there are many complex diseases on your planet at this time. But within that complexity there is a simplicity that can be "unraveled," thereby bringing things back to their original form. This is what we learned from Jesus: healing is simply the return to an aligned state of being in conformity with divine will. Jesus' healing methods are very simple in scope but profound in demonstration.

Jesus introduces Divine Mother's healing power

Of all of the teachings Jesus promoted, none was more startling to us than his depiction of the Holy Divine Mother, the source for all of life. Jesus was very much encircuited in her, which is perhaps the reason why he displayed such strong affinity, respect, and connection with the women disciples. He loved the Holy Mother Spirit and was very devoted to her. He helped us realize how vital these divine feminine qualities are to the fabric of all life. Again, this was quite startling to learn.

In our environment of living in Palestine under Roman rule, human life was devalued. We lived within a conqueror-and-slave mentality. As you know, women were relegated to the role of not having a voice, citizenship—or in some mindsets, the right to even exist. So when Jesus revealed to us the reality of our Divine Mother, can you imagine how liberating and enlightening this was for us to hear? Can you envision how thrilled we were by this good news that we had a Divine Mother who loved us, understood us, and who certainly did not judge us on the mere fact that we were female?

Jesus always showed deep respect for how women thought and engaged with one another, with our children, and with our menfolk. This alone provided a basis for gaining more commitment to our practice in ministry.

And he himself demonstrated qualities of motherliness even though he was a virile man who exuded a very powerful energy. Yet he was always gentle. He was approachable. He was nurturing. Yes, at times he exercised a powerful male strength when he was preaching, teaching, and when he chose to correct an individual. But for the most part he was gentle and engaging, especially with those poor souls who needed a gentle touch, a more compassionate outlook on life, and very tender understanding.

In your time of global spiritual awakening, our Divine Mother is pouring forth her mercy, love, and compassion so that all of her children can engage with this Holy Mother Spirit that Jesus so vividly and generously portrayed.

Over time, the men began to see the fruits of our "family-style" compassion. This legacy of love served as the foundation for the evolving Christian church that came into being a few generations after ours. Along with the men, the women apostles made this worldwide movement possible because, in our case, we embodied the Holy Spirit and her mothering power and provided an environment in which people could thrive as spiritual beings.

Engaging modern women with the gospel mission

We are here to help you appreciate this hidden history, so that more women become empowered as healers, teachers, and ministers of the gospel that Jesus originally taught. We encourage you to spend time with Jesus and let the nurturing essence of his divine personhood embrace you. There is something very significant he has to share with his daughters to empower them and expand them in their own mothering capacities, and we encourage you to pass this on to everyone in your ministries.

Women now have a very important role to play in the evolution of spirituality upon your world. The fact that women have been denied their voice and power indicates what a great distortion in spiritual values has played out in the world's religious traditions, thereby thwarting the true living gospel message of Jesus, which is: membership by all men and women in the family of love under the parenthood of God the Creator.

For those women who are on the cusp of awakening to their inner spiritual potentials, may this account inspire you to live in the power that comes from the Holy Mother Spirit. Allow Jesus to strengthen you when you sit with him and ask for his motherly essence to infuse you.

When our group was formally commissioned by Jesus, this dynamic became even stronger. It reverberated outwardly to attract more people because it spoke to a deep inner hunger for the divine mothering touch, which is an in-born need in humans. The mother-child bond is innate and strong, and when it is not nurtured appropriately, it creates a void within an individual. We were highly effective in our ministry because we filled that void. Unfortunately, as time went on, factors were at play that wore away this influence. Over the generations in the early Christian church, doctrinaire mindsets became more predominant, leading them to set aside the motherly quality that Jesus had passed on to the Women's Corps.

Healing techniques Jesus taught to the Women's Corps

I don't intend to dwell on what happened later in the evolving Christian church. I am speaking rather to its inception and how we played a pivotal role in forming the foundation for something new to be birthed upon the planet today and in the future.

Our access to our Divine Mother infused our healing medicines and techniques. We applied the medicinal substances we had learned about from our mothers and their predecessors, and these were effective up to a certain point. Jesus taught us how to amplify the energies in each substance through the power of prayers to the Holy Mother asking for her presence to pervade it. When we dealt with physical ailments, we would sit as a group over our medicines and pray into them the request that the Holy Mother Spirit's divine action shall prevail. We then applied this intention according to how we were guided by her. We trusted what Jesus taught us about this process because we loved him so dearly and he loved us so completely that we did not doubt what he shared, even though we did not understand all of its implications.

Our work was truly a group effort. The combination of our unified desires to heal was amplified by these infusions of Divine Mother and then directly applied to an individual. As I indicated earlier, we also learned from Jesus to provide a space of safety and compassion to help a person relax their emotions in order to receive our medicines in a state that was more conducive for their reception of the "information" within these medicines. And as we grew in our relationship with Jesus, we improved our ability to provide a peaceful and sacred container in which a person could heal. These were not miraculous cures such as Jesus sometimes performed. We simply elevated people to perceive the higher truths Jesus taught us or receive medicines infused with Divine Mother's energies.

While this "energetic" approach is coming back to life in your advanced cultures, it has a long way to go. Modern medicine does not yet comprehend the principle of the life force of plants and the devitalization of the planet's energy system due to your misuse of its natural healing properties. It is very fortunate that this ancient knowledge is now experiencing a revival.

My particular interest was in healing with natural substances. When I applied them in ministering to the physical body, I also ministered in the Spirit. Other women had other roles to play within the Corps: For example, you have heard the account of Sister Joanna, who acted as a procurer of needed supplies, and of Nasanta, who was an expert in herbal medicine. Other women had other roles to play in our public ministry, including leading, teaching, or preaching. We all had our strengths and our frailties. Jesus amplified those talents that were most beneficial for our development as ministers. Simply being around him invigorated the inner strength and ability in each woman.

You now have access to him through your own Spirit of Truth, and his presence can be just as powerful—perhaps even more so because there is a vast field of collective awareness of Jesus world-wide.

As with the other women, I was able to work more effectively as a healer through the inner qualities he amplified in me. I came to understand the imprint of natural substances and their synergistic relationships with the human body. We applied them as tonics, ointments, or salves. When we prayed into the healing quality of each natural substance, Holy Mother activated its effectiveness and we were often able to witness a healing response.

While some ailments were beyond our capacity, we also witnessed spontaneous changes in the physical condition of some individuals. Again, these were not "miracle cures" as you call them. Instead, we learned from Jesus how the substances of the earth are calibrated to support the healing process, and that under the right conditions they will be efficacious.

Our ministries catalyze the early church

I gained and grew much from this training. One of the reasons we were successful in building the foundation of the early Christian church is that our reputation as healers and teachers grew. Women would bring their infirm family members to us for ministration. We would hold them in such a bond of love and compassion that they could relax and receive what we were imparting through the power of the Holy Spirit. This had a profound impact upon individuals, and it drew people into our fold because they gained an experience of positive faith and a tangible relationship to the power of the Spirit.

Now, did everyone respond in the same way? No! That would be improbable to say the least. But there were those who had enough spiritual curiosity and hunger to stay and learn. And we were then able to minister to them at another level through preaching and teaching.

The many, many individuals who experienced our ministry added to our growing foundation of a community. All we knew was that we were growing our family of love. It felt good. It was warm and it was comforting. Did we all agree upon certain beliefs? Of course not. We each had our own insights and experiences. But that did not supersede the bond of love that grew between us. I say that because, when you help someone heal, a relationship bond is forged. This trust and compassion evolves into understanding and acceptance of one another. Our desire now is to return the modern church to the presence of the Holy Mother Spirit upon which we built a love foundation.

Did we understand what we were doing? Not at all. It was all beyond our level of comprehension. But now that we are in a different state of being, we can look back and see now what Jesus was doing to prepare not only us men and women in Palestine, but to bring about the spread of his teachings worldwide.

In closing my account, let me say that I am deeply grateful for my human life experience. We fervently wish to fortify you with our presence that you may carry on our work and help those who wish to come to Jesus to participate with him in the unfolding adventure of Father-consciousness and Mother-mindedness.

"Whenever he was in our midst my bond with him was so strong that it left me almost speechless, being overcome with the love he emanated."

11

REBECCA

Greetings! My name is Rebecca. I was one of last to join the Women's Evangelistic Corps, coming on a bit later than the first ten. Nevertheless, I was mightily pleased and gratified to become a part of the eminent body of women who were so dedicated to our beloved Master.

My father was Joseph of Arimathea, whom you know as the wealthy man who provided the tomb for Jesus' body after the crucifixion. My father loved Jesus dearly and devotedly. There was nothing he would not do to support Jesus and his ministry, and as a result, my father strongly encouraged me to a become devoted disciple of Jesus. I was elated when the honor was later bestowed upon me to become a member of his Women's Evangelistic Corps.

I was almost the youngest member of this Corps. Jesus was very accommodating to my needs and interests, giving me enough time to comfortably explore where my labors would be of best use.

To say that I was smitten with Jesus underscores my deep love and devotion. Truly, just being in his presence was unlike any experience I have ever had with another person. This was not a romantic or sexual attraction; it was truly a soul-bond. I felt so close to him. Even though I did not see him very much, whenever he was in our midst, my bond with him was so strong that it left me almost speechless, being overcome with the love he emanated.

Other sisters have shared their experiences of being spiritually opened when they were in proximity to Jesus. This did not happen for me quite as starkly, because I believe my father had already transferred to me some of the emotional connection to Jesus that he had expressed in his support for the gospel ministry. Ultimately, my father's deep devotion led me to seek out Jesus and discover how I, too, could support the mission.

I discover the joys of loving service

Jesus had played a prominent role in our family life, both with my parents and my siblings. When he visited us he did not stay for very long, but each time his enormous personality presence always left great and indelible marks upon our minds and hearts and filled our home with his grace. It might be hard to imagine this sort of thing today, because your lives are so filled with gadgets and gizmos that take you away from your relationships and interactions with others. Our family, on the other hand, did not have these distractions. When Jesus was in our home, the place became infused with his love, compassion, and understanding. Our home soon became a place of great love, always providing welcome to believers who were living the gospel teachings.

That's why it felt so natural for me to support Jesus' ministry by becoming involved in the Women's Corps. Helping in the encampment was such an honor for me that I sometimes felt quite insignificant and not up to the task. My sisters supported me regardless as I became more and more comfortable with my place in Jesus' ministry.

My soul was nourished by our common work of providing service to others, and it was natural and simple for me to serve. However, as I observe your current culture, I see how disassociated you can become from one another. In fact, I find it quite jarring to witness the stark contrasts between our two cultures. In our day, we were very devoted to each other. Jesus fostered close loving relationships, helping us to understand the divine dignity within each individual. Because he taught us to listen to each person's story and life experiences, it became easier to minister to them in the Spirit.

My relationship with Jesus and my time in the encampments was one of the best periods of my life. I thrived on being of service in any way I could. I delighted in being with my sisters and sharing the burden of the work that needed to be done. It may be challenging for you to imagine, given your modern-day culture, that our back-breaking tasks involved in ministering to those with maladies of body, mind, and emotion was nevertheless an uplifting experience. Because love and caring for others always pervaded our encampments, the workload of the Women's Corps did not feel burdensome. It was instead joyful.

Whenever I had personal concerns or problems with an individual, I consulted with my sisters, and we would discuss ways to address the situation. Sometimes we sought Jesus' counsel and guidance. He always directed us to go into prayerful meditation with our Spirit to discern the best courses of action. I believe this approach to problem solving was primarily responsible for how loving relationships continued to grow in each encampment. And almost like a byproduct of this method, our ministry spawned a model for the growing Christian church to use for relationship problem-solving.

The many challenges of personal ministry— past and present

All was not perfect in our ministry. We faced many difficulties—for example, certain biases against us from communities who did not align with Jesus. We also encountered challenges from the male apostles who were unsure about our methods. And there were other factors difficult for us to surmount. But we carried on our work with grateful hearts because Jesus had taught us that all was not right on this planet. He explained that he was here to restore a new order of life predicated upon the loving nature of God and the joy of service to humanity. We were all greatly edified by this, especially me because I was so young and still growing as a woman.

Our challenges parallel what you encounter today, especially in the realm of healing. Human needs are great by nature. And yet, many people cannot or do not recognize that they have unmet needs. They allow problems to fester until they reach quite drastic proportions wherein their misery and suffering become greater than it should be. Jesus well understood how the pervasive problems of this planet lead to bad outcomes for those who are weak and poor and are unable to sort out their needs. We learned by observing him how to elicit insights from these individuals that would in turn lead to their unmet needs being fulfilled. Jesus was indeed quite masterful in identifying and touching the real needs of every soul. He also led each person to that deep place where they would discover with certainty they were loved by God.

Because of his influence, we all learned to pay close attention to what people communicated to us about their condition. We searched for that undercurrent of need in order to perceive intuitively what was *not* said. It bears repeating that most people have no true understanding of their fundamental spiritual needs. And yes, of course, it is important to provide for the obvious imperatives such as food, clothing, and shelter. But here I want to emphasize everyone's deeper requirement to appreciate their basic value as a human being. To get at this fundamental need, I learned to listen with the most open heart I could and move beyond a person's pain to help them find that place where the Spirit reveals God's love for them, elevating it to their conscious mind. I honed this skill with practice and time, which became even more effective when it was augmented by the later bestowal of the Spirit of Truth.

The numerous distractions you face in your modern world take you away from making spiritual development a priority. But for us, spiritual growth was based on loving relationships, and we were adept at entering into deep soul connections to each person. As we forged these bonds of friendship, we noticed that people became more content within themselves, even to the point of feeling happiness and well-being.

In our day as in yours, too many people allow contentment to slip away when it is so easily reached if they would only develop more intimacy with others and with the Spirit within.

How our mission continued after Jesus left us

Jesus was like a magnet that drew love and peace into my being. I felt new life coursing through me and amplifying my desire to serve. The joy of service Jesus radiated stayed with me even when he was not present at the encampments, and especially after he left us permanently. The endowment of the Spirit of Truth kept us close to Jesus—fortifying us to continue to grow our healing and spiritual ministry.

My sorrow and grief at Jesus' crucifixion was profound, and for a few days I struggled with hopelessness and despair. When my sisters discovered that the tomb was empty, we were quite mystified as to what could have happened to him. But when he came to us after first appearing to our sister Mary, I was overjoyed that he was still with us, even if only for a very short time.

I find it difficult to describe my astonishment at seeing him in glorified human form. Jesus explained that we, too, would assume this form after we left our physical bodies, which I found very encouraging. I began to lose my dread of dying, which still remains a great mystery to you today. It was immensely liberating to know I would one day be with him again, and that my life would continue to progress on an endless spiritual journey of eternal life.

Soon after the resurrection appearances, the event of Pentecost descended upon us. I cherish my memories of this august day. Those of us who were present in that room, the

Women's Corps, the apostles, and many disciples, all felt a "covering" come over us, but each person experienced this uniquely. I felt elation and a powerful surging desire to go out and minister in Jesus' name, compelled to do so from within by the Spirit.

We needed time to adjust to this amazing new inner reality. But before long, we continued our work with great relish and gusto. As you well know, our growing movement after Pentecost was not well received by all. There soon came a time when we, as followers of Jesus, clashed with the Jewish ecclesiastical authority. In addition, social unrest was fomented by the Zealots who wanted to liberate us from Rome. Despite all the political maneuvering, we persevered in our previous ministry to the infirm and the spiritually hungry.

The political chaos around us instilled a certain fear and anxiety, which for me greatly contrasted with my profound experiences with Jesus. I was steadied by my faith for what was to come. Many of us were killed because of our stalwart belief in Jesus, and I was one of them. It is not so important for me to share with you my physical demise as it is to impart the awareness that death is simply a transitional state of being. I look back now at my departure from this planet as a time of great joy when I rejoined my beloved Master.

He greeted me upon my awakening in my new life. You cannot imagine the immense love that I experienced coming from him. One day you, too, will discover the truth of the majesty of his being and the glory of his love. Human emotions have the capacity to experience great love. It expands as we undergo various stages of experiential spiritual growth. Each stage opens you up to experiences of even greater fulfillment in terms of who you are and the purposes for which you have been created.

I can honestly say that, when I was awakened at this higher level, all of the pain, anxiety, and uncertainty I experienced as a human washed away. Now my eternal adventure is upon me. I look back with such fondness and gratitude for my experiences with Jesus in being a member of his corps of women who set about to follow him. We did not know we were changing the world!

May my life experience give inspiration to others who seek a life rich in the Spirit. May you draw closer to Jesus' love for you and his support for finding your way to elevate your own humanity. We are happy to encourage your efforts in healing our world. Yes, there is much work to be done. Jesus is here to guide you and answer every sincere prayer to be of service to the higher purposes of this planet. May you be fruitful in what you achieve!

"Even though Jesus was male in body and appearance, he appealed to me beyond gender. His understanding of women was quite astonishing."

10

RUTH

My name is Ruth, and I'm pleased to share my story of how I became attached to Jesus and the Women's Evangelistic Corps. I was doubly blessed to also be exposed to Jesus through my father, Matthew Levi, whom as you know was one of his apostles. At first, my family was quite startled when my father shared his desire to be one of his ministers. And then, one memorable day, Jesus came to our home to instruct my father about the gospel mission, and my father was generous enough to allow us children to listen to what Jesus had to say.

This day was a turning point in my inner life. I could sense Jesus' profound love for humanity. I could feel his compassion for those who had been caught up in superstitions and fears that obfuscated their awareness of the Father's Indwelling Spirit. After hearing this teaching and the many other things he said that day, my heart turned toward Jesus.

When my father later went about his travels with Jesus and the other apostles, he came back with much to share.

He regaled us with stories about the impact Jesus had on individuals, not only through his spoken words but because of the generosity of spirit Jesus extended to one and all. As a result, I became increasingly drawn in. I knew that this was a powerful human who had something very grand and glorious to offer. I was even quite envious of my father, who had direct access to him. I wanted, like my father, to be one of the disciples, especially when I learned that women were joining the encampment of followers of Jesus.

Joining the Corps with my father's encouragement

My father encouraged me to inquire about these women. But being so young, I did not at first know what I had to offer. I only knew that they were ministering to spiritual seekers and dispensing medicines and words of encouragement to those who needed healing. Upon visiting the camp, I witnessed how these women gave of themselves so freely to others. As I reflected on their work, I found this type of service to others to be quite liberating.

I was mightily touched by the plight of the people who sought Jesus, those reaching out for healing, love, compassion, and understanding. As we all know, the aura around the Master was so powerfully magnetic that it drew very large numbers of people to him, and of course, I was one of them!

As I said, my interest in Jesus was also heightened by my father's devotion. My father was known in the region as a tax collector, a job with low social standing that many resented. Our family and my father were tainted by this association, unlike some of the other members of the Evangelistic Corps who started out with a higher status. But my father was a courageous man. He deeply influenced me by his decision to become Jesus' apostle, despite being derided about his previous work.

I learned from my father to rise above ridicule and disdain. I was further strengthened by being around Jesus, who elevated my sense of self—just as he had done for my father. And the women devoted to Jesus did not look upon me with disdain, perhaps because Jesus had also elevated *their* self-concepts as women. My father was very frank in helping me appreciate that I was so much more than his daughter or a mere member of a religious group or tradition. Because of all these things, I soon began to experience inner promptings based on my new-found dignity as daughter of God.

Even though Jesus was male in body and appearance, he appealed to me beyond gender. His understanding of women was quite astonishing. He never held to the stigmas about the feminine as many of his male apostles had. Even my father sometimes entertained those old ideas about women being inferior. But he did much in one lifetime to overcome his bias, especially when he saw how effective the women were in our healing ministry based on what Jesus taught us.

Jesus' profound impact on my life

Jesus elevated my self-awareness beyond my social status, and this enhancement gave me the courage to join the Women's Corps. Even though I was very young in comparison to some other women, the group did not treat me like a child. Here again was another example of Jesus' magnanimity. He did not regard age, gender, social status, racial inheritance, or religious tradition as a limiting factor in how he regarded a person. The purity of a person's soul was what he most cared about. His loving demeanor and the way he comported himself around others was so unusual and so impressive.

Because of what Jesus catalyzed in me and my father, I was primed to follow in his footsteps. Finally, the time came when I made an earnest attempt to share with him what was on my heart and mind, and that experience was one of the most profound I have ever had. Even now in my afterlife, it remains one of my most compelling, interesting, and uplifting moments. I cannot convey with words how his love moved me to a place I did not know existed within. I felt my own inner truth for the first time, but even this is an understatement because it was so much more than that. This inner revelation of my status as a daughter of God changed me utterly. It was electrifying, as if every pore and fiber in my being was vitalized and awakened to something new.

I immediately decided to follow him no matter where it would lead, and this decision was based on the greater sense of self he had sparked in me. I share this with you because it is time for everyone on earth to open to the goodness within human nature. If my words can express the majesty and the beauty of this experience, then I will have accomplished my task of expressing what it was like to be around Jesus. I was able to resonate with a truth so noble and good that that I wanted to be like Jesus in every sense of the word.

I shared my conversion experience with my sisters, who had all felt the same thing in their own way. Our common soul-bond created a sacred container that allowed people to feel held, thereby enhancing their ability to find this blessed space within themselves. As a result, very many of the people we ministered to opened up their inner life to discover the presence of the Creator within them. Our encampments allowed everyone to feel a capacity to live life in a way that none of us had ever before experienced.

When Jesus preached, his words were like honey and a balm to the heart. Even though he spoke in many parables, the loving energy behind those words carried a tonal quality that was deeply resonating. No other person I have ever known offered such a profound expression of truth. It was so powerful! So meaningful and uplifting! For some, this upliftment lasted only a short time, while others returned home because they could not understand what it all meant. But that did not matter to me or our other sisters. We simply went about our ministrations as devotedly as we could, staying loyal to what Jesus taught us to achieve.

As I said earlier, Jesus forged our bond of relationship to the Indwelling Spirit of God, which was new to me. You can only imagine how my sisters and I relished this newfound relationship that Jesus so masterfully evoked in each of us. The result was that each woman's unique personality combined to create a very tight-knit and loving container in which to minister to those who came to us. That was able to occur because we had been woven into the foundation and fabric of love, which provides a safe place for people to feel supported and validated at the depth of their beings. Not everyone was able to appreciate this, but those who did had their lives forever changed.

My training and my growing
appreciation of Divine Mother

At first, most of my time was spent being trained or in assisting other ministers. For example, I helped my sisters distribute healing medicines for the infirm. I was also one of the observers on hand whenever Jesus was present in the encampments, going about healing and ministering. I made a point of closely watching how Jesus and the women spoke to and listened to individuals. I was especially captivated by how the Master was able to zero in on a person and listen to them with his heart, and I also observed how the women emulated Jesus. These experiences especially helped me become a more sympathetic listener. I learned to hold my tongue and instead receive people with an open heart and mind.

I continued to grow in my appreciation of how Jesus ministered to those who came before him. I marveled at his ability and especially his compassionate understanding. My sisters have shared with you their astonishment at how he ministered, which also deeply impacted me. He often seemed so motherly to me; he seemed to convey the largesse of a mother's love.

When I asked him about this one day, he replied by teaching me about the feminine presence of Deity and how it could pervade the human mind and heart. He shared how her presence is like a sustaining and nurturing mother who has great concern for the welfare of her children, and how she is actually the embodiment of the life energies animating all living things upon a planet.

Because he taught us these things, a great revelation of the Divine Mother began to burn within us. My sisters have already shared that we spent time discussing this truth and sitting in quiet meditation to discern her presence. As far as I know, Jesus did not articulate his own divine relationship with our Holy Spirit Mother as his co-equal consort, which I later learned about in my afterlife. Now, as I look back upon my human life experiences, I can see that his intimate relationship to Divine Mother enabled him to radiate that motherly comforting essence.

Regardless of how we understood it at first, it was all so marvelous to behold! Truly we rejoiced when he spoke to us about her. We learned that, as women, we all have an innate bond with the Mother Spirit who gives us the ability to be the life-giving nurturers and caretakers of human life. Her womb of life is shared with us at a human level. We were uplifted to learn this truth, which was yet another example of how Jesus reinforced our status as daughters of divine dignity.

I grew closer and closer to our Divine Mother. There were even times when I could feel her speak directly into my heart. After I was fully trained and felt these stirrings become bolder in my ministrations, I always stayed close to her. Her motherly presence was always very comforting to my heart and soothing to my mind.

How the Pentecostal Spirit energized my mission

Even though I experienced tremendous grief at Jesus' passing, the Holy Mother especially supported me through that sorrowful time. My sisters and I felt her holding us together, even as we became very unsure about how to continue the Master's ministry. Many other things transpired in our inner lives during that period between Jesus' crucifixion and ascension. As I look back now, I believe that we were being prepared for something quite extraordinary.

My experience of Pentecost was very significant, even though we had previously been taught that the power of Spirit evolves gradually upon a world; for example, Jesus had explained this reality to us when he discoursed about the effects of eradicating sin. Prior to leaving us, he uplifted our frame of reference in this way, yet this instruction pales in comparison to what we experienced as we adapted to the new-found power that was poured out upon us. The Pentecostal Spirit was far more than mere words; when these living divine energies infused us, we all immediately knew we were being energized to go out and minister the gospel message, his kinship message of sonship, daughtership, and fraternity. Our realization was all the more enhanced because of our love and devotion to Jesus and the ideals he taught.

My own inner light was magnified many times, and I felt a fervent desire to spread this message of love wherever and with whomever I could. It was more than a calling. It was something I *had* to do. I still had a choice, but to me this seemed like the *only* choice. Nothing else would satisfy my soul. Nothing else could give me such meaning and purpose. Even now he calls on his children to awaken those who are ready in heart and soul to receive this message.

My final exhortations

The material aspects of my life are insignificant compared to my spiritual experiences. After Pentecost, I lived the rest of my life with purpose, meaning, and value. What more can a person ask for? Jesus gave me life, and it was abundant. He extends this same abundance to each and every one of his children in all the worlds in his dominion, but especially to us of this world, for he knows full well how we have suffered. When his graciously offered invitation speaks in your heart, the only possible answer you can give is, "Yes! I receive you and I follow you."

I have nothing more to add, dear ones. How I made the transition to the next life is not important. What is important is how I lived the life he gave me, and that I lived it to the fullest degree. Now it is up to you to do the same should you have the heart and soul to enter into this great mission.

Let our stories reverberate in your heart and know that we are here to uplift you so that you may experience Jesus in the way we did. May you continue the work we so faithfully began with our whole minds, hearts, souls.

"This is one of the greatest gifts he gave all humanity:
acknowledging our special power as women."

12

SUSANNA

I am Susanna, who served as the elected leader of the Women's Evangelistic Corps. I'll begin my story by sharing my early life experience as a female raised in the Jewish religious tradition. As you know, the role of girls and women was highly circumscribed in those days. As a young girl, I knew there would come a time when I would move from the authority of my father to that of the husband selected for me. I was dutiful in that regard, and when the time came for me to be married, I entered into the relationship with about the same emotional reaction as many young women of those days: more or less with resignation. The obligation to carry out my duty had been driven into me. My parents selected a teacher of the Jewish religious tradition for me to wed as his life partner.

We lived in Capernaum, and I was aware of Jesus when he lived in our town as a member of the community. At some point, I became aware that strange things began to happen around him and that there was buzz about his unusual activities. It seemed very odd to me when he began to gather not only male apostles, but also disciples who followed him and listened to the messages he preached. My husband was curious at first, going out in search of him to learn about what he taught. When my husband returned to share some of the things Jesus preached, I could tell he was highly agitated yet quite impacted by Jesus' charming personality. My husband acknowledged that Jesus' demeanor was very compelling, but he felt conflicted because his teachings were not consistent with my husband's beliefs and training.

For my own part, I was a bit suspect of Jesus initially. However, as his notoriety began to spread, I gathered some of my women friends to listen to him when he spoke in the synagogue. You'll recall that women were shielded from the larger worship environment in the synagogue, being sequestered behind screens so we could not be seen. We could only peer out and get glimpses of Jesus in outline. In spite of this barrier, when he spoke I could feel something like an electrifying charge in his words that seemed to float on an air current and enter right into my soul. After that experience, I began to absorb his message. I breathed in his essence, and something stirred in me that changed my life.

The first stirrings of my spiritual awakening

I did not know what to make of this early encounter, but I knew his message contrasted with what I had been taught growing up. He proclaimed a more advanced idea of human goodness and potential, and his words altered my perspective on life. But I found it very difficult to share this discovery with my husband, who did not relate to Jesus in the same way.

I kept these things inside except for my ongoing discussions with the women accompanying me to his public talks. We found Jesus' nature to be so sympathetic that when he spoke it always touched our hearts. Much later, I understood he was speaking directly to the soul in order to awaken something deep within.

This eventually led me to the encampment which arose around him, where I had many discussions with the sisters. What most came to the fore was their awareness that women have value and merit in the sight of God. I could see that these women perceived this truth at a deep level and also as an emotional awareness. And it was this teaching about women that marked the beginning of my liberation and led me to come out from under the authoritarian control of my father and my husband.

I did my best to continue to be a dutiful wife. I held my tongue and did not share my perceptions. I maintained my position outwardly, but inwardly the influence of Jesus' teachings was, as I said, altering my perspective both on life and on the role of women in society.

Please bear in mind that your twenty-first century perspective is vastly different than ours. Jesus stirred an inner sense of my right to exist as a human being, and as a female, who had something very important to contribute. This was new to us as women. This novel idea rose up within my heart, lifting me to a place where I no longer felt unworthy of God's love. I was beginning to see myself as a vital and important part of God's great plan.

My decision to follow Jesus

A period intervened between this realization and the time when I made the decision to follow the Master wherever he went. Fortunately, many of my obligations to my husband and children had already been fulfilled due to the ages of my young ones who were then entering into marriage relationships or careers to support their families.

My husband continued to be one of the more prominent teachers in our community, which made it difficult to separate myself from being acknowledged as his wife. However, I knew I had to move beyond that circumscribed function and begin to play a leadership role with the women of the encampment. I was most gratified when my husband finally recognized my devotion to Jesus and my sincere desire to join the women doing good works within the encampment, and he relented. He gave me permission to follow what was in my heart.

Jesus' reputation grew as he traveled about, engaged in public preaching and healing. As the numbers of his followers swelled, it became obvious that their physical needs required attention. Several of our women moved into the physical care of those women, children, elderly, and infirm.

I soon became involved with helping these people receive nourishment, medicines, and of course, spiritual counsel. You have heard from our other sisters how Jesus spent time with and ministered to needy individuals. He taught us to observe and then emulate his ministrations to those suffering in mind and body, and after a while we were emboldened to follow his example. And during this time some of my creative gifts began to show themselves more fully to the women.

I begin to exercise my leadership and organizational skills

I had managed quite a large household, so this long experience was easily translated into organizing the work requirements of the encampment. The women who had begun to organize the work recognized my skills and elected me as their leader because of my ability to organize and encourage people in their tasks. I was able to catalyze a very cohesive bond in our ministry as we addressed the material problems of those to whom we ministered as well as the needs of their minds and souls, which we considered more pressing.

Thus began a wonderful time of growth. Fortunately, my ministry did not interfere with my home life. My husband witnessed the good works of the Women's Corps, and although he did not fully embrace Jesus' teachings, he recognized the value of our ministry. While I was around him, I still could not fully express my embrace of Jesus' teachings, so I kept them mostly hidden in my heart.

That all changed when I was with my sisters working in the encampments. My heart expanded each time! The love Jesus catalyzed in me found full and free expression in my ministry. I also experienced sisterly kinship as we grew together and increasingly recognized what we women could accomplish as a group. I believe Jesus purposely evoked a firm soul-bond among the women, harmonizing us in a way that our greatest gifts expressed themselves as a synergistic whole.

The rising role of women as daughters of God

In those days I learned a very important life lesson about the nature of women. At first, we didn't even recognize that our vast collective power was being denied due to our religious mores and traditions. Jesus changed all that by bringing us together in such way that validated us as a group and as women. I believe Jesus knew beforehand that he would commission a group of female representatives of the gospel. And to me, this is one of the greatest gifts he gave all humanity: acknowledging our special power as women.

It soon became apparent that our loving environment was a powerfully attractive container in which others could easily engage. Love cannot be confined in a material vessel; it carries an expansive, elastic quality of divinity that seeks out those in need of nurturing and succor.

Our women's group grew into a foundation of love that, as you have heard, later grew into the early Christian church. The church changed into something different later, yet its true origins were the love and validation we expressed to each individual at the soul level.

After Jesus left us, we felt scattered because we lost his anchoring presence. Some women elected to stay in their hometowns. Others decided to accompany the male apostles in their travels, and it is noteworthy that these women brought along with them our technique of creating a loving environment to augment the preaching success of the men.

Once we were all encircuited by the Spirit of Truth during the festival of Pentecost, our new connection to Jesus supplanted certain theological tensions we had been feeling. Initially, our loving synergy prevailed over intellectual dissension. Unfortunately, what ensued in the Christian church was the relegation of women's role to a secondary position.

During the early years, our loving foundation of spiritual kinship was strong enough to foster a growing interest in Jesus. Later, the growing gospel teaching centered more around Jesus' personality and resurrection, and as you know, it was this teaching that spread around the Levant and into the Roman Empire. His magnificent messages of faith and service took more of a back seat.

When in retrospect we recall and trace the historical evolution of the Christian church, we can recognize that the foundation of love laid down by the ministry of the Women's Corps fostered greater receptivity to Jesus' teachings. But again, our achievement did not last due to the various interpretations of his teachings that set aside his exhortation to have faith in God and lovingly serve humanity. Yet, this original foundation of his gospel is still alive and now awaiting its re-emergence and re-introduction by people who are living in his love and sharing it with anyone ready to embrace what he truly came to demonstrate—the Parenthood of God and the loving fraternity of the family of humanity.

The modern-day expression of Jesus' gospel

Once this recognition of the gospel becomes more readily acknowledged, the world will witness its expansion and further expression. And your present-day culture is well on its way to doing this. Our hope is that by telling our stories, we will help people recognize an even deeper level of Jesus' message. Again I say, it is now time for the loving foundation established by the Women's Corps to find new expression throughout the Christian church and become more fully disseminated.

What we women created is still there in etheric historical records. Now is the time for this record to come forth and catalyze a new awareness in those people who profess belief in Jesus. He is even now waiting to touch each person with his love and remove their feelings of unworthiness and guilt. He wishes to validate in each person the divine dignity within by igniting their souls so that they are born again of the Spirit.

We hope you allow Jesus' love to speak volumes to your soul as you read our stories. As this message gains greater presence in the world's consciousness, it will lead more individuals to the wellspring of the eternal truths Jesus taught. We are here to help your world remember this component of Jesus' gospel. And do not doubt that the torch is being passed to another generation of those ready to step into a relationship with Jesus that builds the growing community of believers in the true gospel message of faith and service.

I end my story by informing you that I was able to leave my human body and for my soul to ascend without having to be a victim of persecution. Unfortunately, this fate befell some of my sisters, as you have been told. When the time came to leave my body, I departed with such an open heart, full of the joy of knowing I would reunite with our beloved Master.

His presence is alive upon your planet, and now it is time for others to continue the work he commissioned us to achieve. Our initial achievements will always be there to support what is now coming forth from new generations of female apostles. I leave you in the hope that our story will inspire you to live a life of loving service and spread the true gospel message as Jesus intended for one and all on this beautiful world.

AUTHOR'S EPILOGUE

Following in the Footsteps of the
Original Women's Corps

I am blessed and grateful for my association with our twelve sisters. My heart is deeply touched by their love for and devotion to Jesus. I have been thrilled to learn how he inspired and unified them to become a special corps, as described for the first time in *The Urantia Book*. As conveyed in their stories, their dedication to serving others turned them into a vibrant team of ministry. They were true champions—mighty daughters of God with the courage to break out of the narrow roles of their societal conditioning. What is perhaps most exciting to me is their call for modern-day women to become spiritual healers for our planet, to replicate and build upon the model of ministry they established so long ago through the power of divine love.

Because of their inspiring call, I have made a commitment to emulate the Twelve in my own spiritual ministry. I have created a modern-day Women's Evangelistic Corps at my Institute of Christ Consciousness and we also advocate that other women join us by following in the footsteps of the original corps.

Our particular approach is to provide a loving environment for people to receive the healing Jesus wishes for all of his children. Our corps is dedicated to uplifting those who are ready to reach the core essence of their divine dignity. Our aim is to move them beyond the common feeling of unworthiness and awaken their God-given potential to grow spiritually. We welcome others to join our effort, women like *yourself* who feel ready to create a corps to achieve their own unique ministry objectives.

In fact, I believe the present crisis of our world calls for *thousands* of women to respond to the call of Spirit to become apostles. Because of the challenges we face today, Jesus and our Divine Mother are sending us the spiritual power required to save our troubled world from the unjust structures of the past. These divine energies can support you to become an apostle now!

Therefore, I encourage *you* to start your own Evangelistic Women's Corps in your own way, just as I have done. To assist you, my institute provides training for aspiring women to become leaders of their own groups of ministers. Please contact me to learn how you may participate in this great revival of women as spiritual healers and leaders, or use the link provided below.

Looking ahead, I believe one day there will be apostolic women's corps all over the world. We see evidence of women standing up everywhere, even in countries that have violently suppressed their voices. As I said, this is now possible because Jesus' Spirit of Truth and Mother's Holy Spirit are active everywhere, and if women could be apostles under Jesus then, why not now?

Each of us has spiritual potential that naturally responds to feeling loved. The women have explained how Jesus activated their dormant potential through his love, uplifting them by seeing into their souls and giving them the courage and motivation to express it. Our new ministry replicates this dynamic process to open a person's inner door for true self-perception and God-consciousness that can also catalyze various kinds of healing. Your ministry can do such things as well.

Our new Women's Evangelistic Corps, like that of our ancient sisters, is also dedicated to our Divine Mother. As Co-creator with Jesus, she embodies the feminine divine ideals of the Spirit. She enfolds us in her womb so that we feel secure enough to activate spiritual ideals through pursuing the kind of ministry Jesus modeled.

Our Mother's personality is contactable. Each of us needs our Holy Mother Spirit as much as we need our Creator Father. Men need their Mother as much as women need their Father to bring about a greater balance so that a genuine male-female synergy can function. Readers of this book have learned from the Twelve how this balance of the genders is the underlying foundation of a strong and healthy social culture.

Ultimately, I believe the gospel of Jesus provides the value system we need to transform our social institutions. When love for humanity and for all of life are the guiding principles for social life, there is a natural tendency toward social equality, compassion, fairness, and justice for all. By infusing these dynamics into our cultures, we are in a more favorable position to align with the Spirit. It is time to liberate ourselves from what has plagued human evolution for so many millennia.

Even though sincere Christian women have always reached for the high level of spiritual ministry that the Twelve achieved, this particular time on our planet calls for a greater replication of their ancient model. Today may be the most opportune moment in history for men and women to tap into the synergy that the original women apostles created in their devotion to Jesus. His gospel is the surest way for humanity to overcome its dark history, leading us into a glorious destiny beyond our imaginations that future generations will fulfill.

It is my fondest hope that these stories will touch both men and women in a deep place of truth-recognition. May it inspire more people to respond to Jesus' inner call, thereby bringing these hidden dimensions of his gospel into modern-day expression. More than ever, we need people committed to developing loving relationships, that is, to be forgiving, understanding, and compassionate regarding the frailty of human nature. *We can do this* by living according to the spiritual principles of Jesus and deepening our relationship with our Creators. One day our social order will be based upon the divine principles of love, fairness, equality, and justice for all, resulting in a society that is harmonious and beautiful to behold. Then, as our sisters say, we will have achieved the dreams of our hearts.

In loving service,

Donna D'Ingillo
Delray Beach, Florida

Institute of Christ Consciousness
www.institutechristconsciousness.org
donna@institutechristconsciousness.org

ACTIVATE YOUR OWN WOMEN'S CORPS

Learn more at this link:

https://www.institutechristconsciousness.org/
womens-evangelistic-corps.html

Donna D'Ingillo is a lifelong student of *The Urantia Book* and one of the first full-time ministers of the expanded gospel of Jesus based on the Urantia Revelation. A renowned pioneer in celestial contact for over three decades, she is also the founder and executive director of the Institute of Christ Consciousness. In addition to an extensive spiritual healing and counseling ministry with individuals, she conducts workshops and seminars and hosts popular online sessions each week in which she leads groups in worship, prayer, and global healing. Donna's previous acclaimed titles are *Teach Us to Love* (2011) and *Divine Mother, Divine Father* (2016).

Printed in the USA
CPSIA information can be obtained
at www.ICGtesting.com
JSHW022206270923
49290JS00006B/23